Railway law for "the man in the train" : chiefly intended as a guide for the travelling public on all points likely to arise in connection with the railways.

George E. T. Edalji

The Making of Modern Law collection of legal archives constitutes a genuine revolution in historical legal research because it opens up a wealth of rare and previously inaccessible sources in legal, constitutional, administrative, political, cultural, intellectual, and social history. This unique collection consists of three extensive archives that provide insight into more than 300 years of American and British history. These collections include:

Legal Treatises, 1800-1926: over 20,000 legal treatises provide a comprehensive collection in legal history, business and economics, politics and government.

Trials, 1600-1926: nearly 10,000 titles reveal the drama of famous, infamous, and obscure courtroom cases in America and the British Empire across three centuries.

Primary Sources, 1620-1926: includes reports, statutes and regulations in American history, including early state codes, municipal ordinances, constitutional conventions and compilations, and law dictionaries.

These archives provide a unique research tool for tracking the development of our modern legal system and how it has affected our culture, government, business – nearly every aspect of our everyday life. For the first time, these high-quality digital scans of original works are available via print-on-demand, making them readily accessible to libraries, students, independent scholars, and readers of all ages.

The BiblioLife Network

This project was made possible in part by the BiblioLife Network (BLN), a project aimed at addressing some of the huge challenges facing book preservationists around the world. The BLN includes libraries, library networks, archives, subject matter experts, online communities and library service providers. We believe every book ever published should be available as a high-quality print reproduction; printed on-demand anywhere in the world. This insures the ongoing accessibility of the content and helps generate sustainable revenue for the libraries and organizations that work to preserve these important materials.

The following book is in the "public domain" and represents an authentic reproduction of the text as printed by the original publisher. While we have attempted to accurately maintain the integrity of the original work, there are sometimes problems with the original work or the micro-film from which the books were digitized. This can result in minor errors in reproduction. Possible imperfections include missing and blurred pages, poor pictures, markings and other reproduction issues beyond our control. Because this work is culturally important, we have made it available as part of our commitment to protecting, preserving, and promoting the world's literature.

GUIDE TO FOLD-OUTS MAPS and OVERSIZED IMAGES

The book you are reading was digitized from microfilm captured over the past thirty to forty years. Years after the creation of the original microfilm, the book was converted to digital files and made available in an online database.

In an online database, page images do not need to conform to the size restrictions found in a printed book. When converting these images back into a printed bound book, the page sizes are standardized in ways that maintain the detail of the original. For large images, such as fold-out maps, the original page image is split into two or more pages

Guidelines used to determine how to split the page image follows:

• Some images are split vertically; large images require vertical and horizontal splits.
• For horizontal splits, the content is split left to right.
• For vertical splits, the content is split from top to bottom.
• For both vertical and horizontal splits, the image is processed from top left to bottom right.

RAILWAY LAW

FOR

THE "MAN IN THE TRAIN"

RAILWAY LAW &c.

FOR

THE "MAN IN THE TRAIN"

CHIEFLY INTENDED AS A GUIDE FOR THE
TRAVELLING PUBLIC ON ALL POINTS LIKELY TO
ARISE IN CONNECTION WITH THE RAILWAYS

BY

GEORGE E. T. EDALJI

SOLICITOR

Second Class Honours, Solicitors' Final Examination, November, 1898,
Birmingham Law Society's Bronze Medallist, 1898

LONDON

EFFINGHAM WILSON

ROYAL EXCHANGE

1901

[Entered at Stationers' Hall]

PREFACE.

THERE seems to be no branch of the law regarding which the public labour under greater delusions than that affecting their rights and liabilities when travelling upon the railway and in matters relating thereto.

Most people, whilst being aware that railway companies have a long list of bye-laws and regulations printed in their time tables and exhibited at the stations, will readily admit that far from ever having considered the validity of such bye-laws, or the right of the companies to make same, they are altogether in the dark concerning the very existence of many of them.

Ask any ordinary traveller what is his legal position in case he starts his journey without a ticket, travels beyond the station to which he has booked, rides in superior class, smokes in a non-smoking carriage; smashes a window; persists in entering a full compartment, finds a purse on the company's property, or, last, but not least, wishes to imbibe of stimulating beverages in the refreshment room at some railway station on Sunday!—and it will be found that he has some very vague and incorrect notions on the matter.

This little book, then, is intended as a guide to all points on railway law likely to arise in everyday life, and as such I trust it may be of interest and use to those for whom it is mainly intended—namely, the travelling public

Not, therefore, having written primarily for the profession, I have (except in some few instances) omitted all references to cases, etc. ; at the same time I hope the book may find its way into many lawyers' offices.

In conclusion, I need only add that I have endeavoured to deal with the subject in as plain and interesting a manner as possible, and that any hints or suggestions for a future edition will be carefully considered

G. E T. E

54 Newhall Street,
Birmingham, *December*, 1900.

CONTENTS.

CHAPTER I

BYE-LAWS AND THEIR VALIDITY . PAGE
1

CHAPTER II

SEASON TICKETS 41

CHAPTER III.

UNPUNCTUALITY OF TRAINS, ETC . . 46

CHAPTER IV.

LUGGAGE . . 62

CHAPTER V

THE CARRIAGE OF CYCLES 82

CHAPTER VI.

ACCIDENTS . . . 85

CHAPTER VII

SOME MISCELLANEOUS POINTS 98

ADDENDA TO CHAPTER III

UNPUNCTUALITY OF TRAINS—"WILFUL MISCONDUCT"
—WHAT IS?—IMPORTANT DECISION

As I am correcting the proofs, it has been held by
His Honour Judge Lumley Smith, Q.C., in the
case of *Phillips v. London, Brighton and South Coast
Railway Company*, that it is not "wilful misconduct" on a railway company's part to neglect to
inform passengers in a train that they would be
unable to proceed for two hours owing to a break-
down on the line; and, consequently, that although
a passenger could prove that if he had been told of
the accident he could have taken a cab and thus
avoided the loss of an important business engagement, he will nevertheless have no right to claim
damages from the company

I believe the plaintiff in this case means to
appeal against what appears a most unfair decision, and I wish him success

Until this decision is overruled, a railway
company will be able with impunity, in case
of a serious accident occurring, to keep their
passengers sitting in the trains for any unlimited
period without informing them as to how long
the detention is likely to last.

RAILWAY LAW

"MAN IN THE TRAIN".

CHAPTER I.

BYE-LAWS AND THEIR VALIDITY.

By the Regulation of Railways Act, 1889,[1] a passenger must, on the request of any authorised servant of the company, either—

(i.) Produce and, if so required, deliver up a ticket showing that his fare is paid; or,

(ii.) Pay his fare from the station from which he (not the train) started ; or,

(iii.) Give his name and address.

A passenger neglecting to do *one* of these three alternatives on request is liable to a fine of £2.

Further, if a traveller having failed either to produce or deliver up a ticket showing that his fare is paid, or to pay his fare, refuses, on request by an officer or servant of the company, to give his name or address, any officer of the company, or

[1] 52 & 53 Vic., cap 57, sec 5.

I

any constable, may detain him till he can be conveniently brought before some justice, or otherwise legally discharged.

It should be observed then—

(*a*) That the £2 penalty is only incurred by passengers failing to do *one* of the three alternatives mentioned.

(*b*) That a passenger cannot be compelled to "deliver up" his ticket, but if he objects for any reason to do so, he must give his name and address.

(*c*) That no traveller can be legally detained, unless he has not only refused to show his ticket or pay the fare, but has also declined to give his name and address.

In the case of *Earl Russell* v. *Great Eastern Railway Co*, heard in 1894, at the Lord Mayor's Court, before the late Recorder of London, Sir Charles Hall, Q C., the facts were that Earl Russell and a friend took third class tickets from Liverpool Street, London, to Cambridge. The journey being made by express train, it was customary to collect tickets before starting Earl Russell and his companion gave up their tickets on demand, but just afterwards, other travellers entering the compartment, and the Earl desiring to discuss a private matter with his friend, they got out and entered another carriage. A ticket collector came up and again demanded their tickets On being told that they had been surrendered, a heated discussion ensued as to the travellers' *bonâ fides*, but beyond being very insolent the collector did nothing.

On his return from Cambridge, Earl Russell booked third class to Liverpool Street, and, remembering his recent disagreeable experience, refused to give up his ticket before departure of the train, saying he would deliver it on completion of the journey

It so happened that the officials at Cambridge were at that time afflicted with the same malady as their brethren in town, namely, extreme irritability of temper, so Earl Russell was told, in the most peremptory manner, that unless the ticket was instantly handed over he would not be permitted to travel by the train

On his still declining to surrender the ticket his luggage was hurled from the train, and he himself threatened with great violence. At the hearing of the action which the Earl brought against the company for assault, the Recorder held there was no power to eject a passenger under such circumstances, and gave judgment for £10 and costs. Leave to appeal was refused

The plaintiff in this case was, no doubt, both legally and morally justified in adopting the course he did : but, whatever a passenger's strictly legal rights may be, few people can have any sympathy with those travellers who, for no reason at all, cause trouble and delay by obstinately refusing to give up their tickets, or by tendering copies in place of the originals.

The point has been raised as to whether a porter is an "officer" of the company possessing power to detain a passenger within the meaning of the

above Act From the use of the words "an officer
or servant" in the earlier part of the enactment,
as distinct from "any officer or any constable" in
the latter part, it appears that a porter is not, in
his capacity of porter simply, an officer having
power to detain. It is possible, however, that at a
small station, where it was a porter's duty to collect
tickets, he might, in the absence of the stationmaster or some other official of higher rank, become,
pro tempore, an officer with power of detention It
was evidently the intention of the legislature to cast
upon some more experienced and responsible person than a porter the very serious duty of having
to decide whether or not a traveller ought to be
detained.

The Act referred to also provides—

(i) That if anyone travels, or attempts to do so,
without having previously paid his fare, and with
intent to avoid payment thereof; or,

(ii) Having paid his fare for a certain distance,
knowingly and *wilfully* proceeds by train beyond
that distance, without previously paying the additional fare for the additional distance, and with the
like intent; or,

(iii.) Having failed to pay his fare, gives a false
name or address to a servant of the company,

He shall be liable to a penalty of £2 for a
first offence, or £20, or, in the court's discretion,
one month's imprisonment for a subsequent
offence

Note carefully that these penalties are *only* incurred by persons who either—

(*a*) Fraudulently travel without tickets with the intention of cheating the company, or,

(*b*) Knowingly and wilfully proceed beyond the station to which they have booked, with the same intention ; or,

(*c*) Give wrong names or addresses.

If a passenger is suspected of giving a wrong name or address he may be detained pending inquiry; but, by so detaining any person, the company run considerable risk, and will be liable to pay damages for false imprisonment should the name and address be ultimately found to be correct, and this although the traveller's conduct may have been such as to reasonably lead one to suppose he was not speaking the truth

Railway companies have statutory powers of making bye-laws for regulating the travelling upon and using of their railways, which bye-laws may impose penalties of not exceeding £5 for each offence

The great principles governing all such bye-laws are—

(i) They must not be repugnant to the laws of the country, and,

(ii.) They must not be unreasonable

Any bye-law transgressing either of these fundamental principles will be utterly void.

Considering the extremely wide powers possessed by railway companies of acquiring the land requisite for their undertaking, in spite of an owner's objection to part with his property, it would certainly be improper to permit them to inconvenience the public by upholding any too stringent bye-laws

Many people, not unnaturally, suppose that because a bye-law is sanctioned by the Board of Trade, and published at all the company's stations (as every bye-law is required to *be* sanctioned and published), the same is therefore valid and binding. but this is a fallacy Broadly speaking, it may be said that no bye-law is valid which, in any form or shape, attempts to impose a penalty on a person who *without fraud* does that which by common or statute law is only punishable when done *with intent to defraud*.

Let us now consider some of the usual bye-laws which, in the case of all railway companies, will be found to be in practically the same words

I may as well begin with a bye-law of the existence of which most travellers will be aware (though as to its legal value I fear many of them are profoundly ignorant) providing that " No passenger will be allowed to enter any carriage used on the railway, or to travel therein, unless furnished by the company with a ticket Every passenger shall show and deliver up his ticket (whether a contract or season ticket or otherwise) to any duly authorised servant of the company whenever required to do so for any purpose. Any passenger travelling without a ticket, or failing or refusing to show or deliver up his ticket as aforesaid, shall be required to pay the fare from the station from which the train originally started to the end of his journey."

Dealing with the latter part of this bye-law first, it will be observed that it offends against both the principles just enunciated regulating the validity of bye-laws, because—

(*a*) It does not allow a traveller the benefit of the three alternatives (namely, to show his ticket, pay the fare, or give his name and address) specified in the Act already mentioned.

(*b*) It is obviously unreasonable in that it attempts to impose the same penalty on a person who for some reason fails to show or give up his ticket as on one who has taken no ticket at all, and the same penalty on the passenger who has come, say, four miles, without a ticket as on him who has come forty.

If, therefore, a passenger has no ticket, he should tender the fare from the station from which he started, paying no heed to the demand for anything further which is sometimes made, as such additional amount is in no way recoverable.[1]

Although a legal tender be refused, the amount thereof must be paid, if the company subsequently apply for it, after deducting the cost of transmission, if any. Should the traveller be sued for the fare, the sum tendered must be paid into court, when the company will have to bear all costs.

In case a ticket is lost or mislaid the passenger should decline to pay again, as the fact of his

---

[1] *L B & S C Railway* v *Watson*, 4 C.P.D , 118, 26 W.R., 856.

already having done so can almost invariably be proved.

Of course payment of the fare should always be refused, and the traveller's name and address given if required, in case the ticket has been previously surrendered in error at a collecting station, as sometimes occurs when tickets are collected for station A, but only examined for stations beyond A. The same course should be adopted when the return half of a ticket has been given up on the outward journey

Dealing with the former part of the bye-law under consideration, it frequently happens that a passenger reaches the station too late to book, but yet in time for the train. Under such circumstances he should avoid the useless practice—prevalent with some people—of immediately apprising the guard of the fact, and abstain from collecting around him as many of the company's servants as possible in order to tell them he has got no ticket. Such a procedure can do neither passenger nor officials any possible good, and will doubtless irritate the latter, and at some stations cause the former to lose his train, for that part of the bye-law prohibiting a traveller from *starting* on his journey without a ticket is perfectly valid. Although a passenger has actually entered the train, he may be removed if he has got no ticket before commencement of the journey (though not, it is submitted, afterwards), and this notwithstanding the fare be tendered.

Turning next to those bye-laws imposing

penalties of not exceeding £2 on passengers who use, or attempt to use, out-of-date tickets, or tickets which have been used on a previous occasion, it will be seen from what has already been said that they are only valid to the extent that such tickets are used with fraudulent design, and it appears from one case, though the point is very doubtful, that a passenger accidentally missing his train, and there being no other train the same day, may travel by the next reasonably available train without paying any additional fare

A return ticket, however, is usually of no avail after expiration of the time stated thereon, although the excess fare (if any) necessary to make the cost of the return ticket equal to what the passenger would have had to pay for two single journey tickets be tendered.

Thus, suppose the single fare from A to B is 1s 6d, and the return fare 2s 8d, a traveller taking a return ticket and paying his 2s 8d cannot strictly use it to return after the time allowed by paying 4d, but will be required to pay the full 1s 6d, the double journey, thus costing him 1s 2d more than if he had taken two single journey tickets. It may be mentioned that in the case of first and second class tickets passengers will always find it cheaper to "book return," and on some lines third class return tickets also are cheaper than two single ones.

Although the mere giving up of an out-of-date return ticket would not in itself be any evidence of fraud, the safer course is to simply state that

the ticket is out of date, at the same time tendering the amount, if any, necessary to make up the
cost of another single journey ticket, in which case
the company will rarely sue for the excess fare.

In the case of *North Staffordshire Railway Co
v Huffam,*[1] defendant travelled with the return
half of a ticket after expiration of the time for
which the same was available   The company
prosecuted him under a bye-law providing that
any passenger using or attempting to use a ticket
for any day on which it was not available should
be liable to a penalty of £2   The company succeeded before the magistrates, Mr Huffam being
convicted   On appeal, however, it was held that
the bye-law was void on the ground that *intent to
defraud* the company was an essential element,
and it was admitted that the fare had been paid in
the first instance, and the company could prove
no fraudulent design   The conviction was accordingly very properly quashed

It has been proposed to pass a short Act making
return tickets available after any length of time, and
surely no harm could be done by extending the period
to, say, one year after the date of issue.   The
passenger having paid for his ticket, in what possible
way can it affect the company when he returns?

It has been argued that the traveller by taking
a return ticket is carried at a lower fare than if he
took two single tickets, and that if he overstays
the time mentioned on the ticket he is getting

[1] [1894] W N, 166, 63 L J.M.C., 225, 10 T., 653

a greater advantage than the company have contracted to give him, and that for such greater advantage he must pay an increased fare. There may be some truth in this contention in so far as it affects first and second class passengers, but seeing that, as has been said, in the case of third class passengers (who form 92 per cent. or more of the travelling public) there is often no advantage in "booking return," it is absurd to subject them to the same restrictions

It must be remembered that a return ticket is granted solely for the purpose of enabling the person for whom the same is issued to travel therewith to and from the stations named thereon, and is not transferable.

A passenger selling or parting with or attempting to sell or part with the return half incurs a penalty of not exceeding £2 ; so also does a person purchasing such half of a return ticket, or travelling or attempting to travel therewith, and the latter will in addition be liable to pay the full ordinary fare from the station at which he commenced his journey

At intermediate stations tickets are only issued conditionally on their being room in the train— at least this is the theory—but in practice, as everyone knows, on lack of room passengers are unceremoniously hustled into the luggage van. If any passenger objects to stand, or ride in the van, he may surrender his ticket and have his money returned.

Passengers obliged to travel in inferior class

owing to overcrowding may obtain a return of the difference between the fares for the respective classes, but the fact of their having to ride in the inferior class should be notified to some servant of the company before completion of the journey, and travellers should decline to give up their tickets till the money due to them is paid, or at any rate eep the numbers of such tickets

The usual bye-law on this subject is so absolutely ludicrous that I cannot refrain from giving it verbatim; it reads as follows —

"At the intermediate stations the fares will only be accepted, and the tickets issued conditionally, that is to say in case there shall be room in the train for which the tickets are issued In case there shall not be room for all, the passengers to whom tickets have been issued for the longest distance shall, if reasonably practicable, have the preference, and those passengers to whom tickets have been issued for the same distance shall, if reasonably practicable, have priority according to the order in which tickets have been issued as denoted by the consecutive numbers stamped upon them The company will not, however, hold itself responsible for such order of preference or priority being adhered to, but the fare, or difference of fare, if the passenger travel by an ordinary train in a class of carriage inferior to that for which he has a ticket, shall be immediately returned on application to any passenger for whom there is no room as aforesaid if the application be made before departure of the train."

A few words of explanation seem desirable as to the meaning of the words "intermediate stations" Of course if we take the word "intermediate" in its strict literal sense as signifying "lying between two points," or "intervening," nearly every station might be said to be "intermediate" Passengers at Birmingham (Snow Hill) who had booked to Paddington would indeed be surprised if they were informed that Birmingham was only an intermediate station because the train had in the first instance started from Shrewsbury or Birkenhead!

I think the words "intermediate stations," as used in this bye-law, must, if any value at all is to be attached to them, mean small stations at which there are no facilities for coping with an inordinately large number of passengers, and where no spare coaches are kept ready for an emergency Such stations as Rugby, Crewe, Chester, etc, could not be said to be intermediate stations, whether the train was originally "made up" at them or not, and in case there was no room it would be the company's duty to put on more carriages or run a special train

It will be noticed that for obvious reasons the company do not in any way bind themselves to comply with the provisions of the bye-law just stated, and indeed the framers thereof must have been aware that it never could be "reasonably practicable" for the company's servants to go through the absurd process of making the inquiries and inspections indicated.

Imagine, for instance, a crowded platform on

some bank holiday, or occasioned by a race meeting or football match, and each train being delayed whilst it was ascertained where every passenger was going and who booked first!

Further, although travellers who could not find room might be able to apply for return of their money "before departure of the train," it would be impracticable to "immediately return" the difference in fares to those persons obliged to travel in an inferior class, even assuming they were in a position to apply for the return thereof at once, and the company could not legally decline to return a fare on the ground of application not being made till after departure of the train

An action for damages lies against a railway company at the suit of any passenger inconvenienced or injured by overcrowding A few years ago a Birmingham barrister sued the London and North-Western Railway Company for damages for inconvenience caused him by the company overcrowding their trains at Stechford Station on three specified dates, and recovered, I believe, five guineas for each occasion

The overcrowding question cropped up again in 1897 at Ilkeston County Court, where the Midland Railway Company sued a Mr. Kennaway for 1s 7d. excess fare in consequence of his having travelled first class with a third class season ticket on 30th June, 1897 Defendant admitted the claim, but counterclaimed for damages for inconvenience and annoyance suffered on two stated occasions by reason of the company at an

intermediate station allowing more than the proper
number of passengers to enter the compartment
in which he was riding. His Honour, Judge
Smyly, gave judgment in Mr Kennaway's favour
for 1s and 1s 6d. respectively on the counter-
claims, and refused the company leave to appeal

A decision which seems rather hard on the
passenger was arrived at by the House of Lords
in the case of *Cobb* v. *Great Western Railway
Co.*[1] about six years ago   The facts were that at
Wellington (Salop) Station sixteen men entered a
compartment constructed to carry only ten persons,
in which compartment Mr Cobb was already a
passenger. The latter was assaulted and robbed
by some of the new comers. The stationmaster
refused to delay the train in order that police,
present in the station, might arrest or search the
men

In the action Mr Cobb brought against the
company to recover compensation for the loss of
his property, the House of Lords, affirming the
decision of the Court of Appeal, held that the
starting of the train was not placing an obstacle
in the way of the recovery of the property of
such a nature as to render the company liable in
damages, and that no sufficient connection had
been shown between the overcrowding and the
loss.

The following moot point has been discussed by
I think the majority of legal debating societies in

---

[1] [1894] *A.C.*, 419 , 63 *L J Q B* , 629

the country, and decided as often the one way as the other :—

"A is in a first class carriage with a first class ticket At Mudulwell Junction the guard fills A's compartment with third class passengers Has A any right of action against the company for damages ? "

I have been unable to find any direct authority on this point, but should say that as the company have for all practical purposes turned the first class carriage into a third class, A would have a good claim against the company for damages for breach of their implied contract to carry him to his destination in a carriage of the description for which they sold him a ticket. The amount of damages recoverable would be the difference between the first and third class fares

It seems not to be generally known that railway companies have a bye-law (which is perfectly valid) providing that any person persisting in entering a compartment containing the full number of passengers which such compartment is constructed to convey, after objection has been made to his so doing by any occupant of the compartment, shall be liable to a penalty of £2 and it would be no defence for anyone so entering a full compartment to prove there was no room elsewhere. An assault case decided in January, 1900, at Marylebone Police Court by Mr. Curtis Bennett is both interesting and instructive, and I therefore give full details thereof, only omitting the parties' names and addresses The complainant stated

that on 27th December (which was holiday time)
he and others filled a first class compartment
when the train left Broad Street. At Highbury
he held the door handle inside to prevent anyone
else entering Then somebody tried to open the
door, and finding it was a lady he allowed her to
come in, at the same time remarking that the
compartment was full

She then commenced to abuse him, and on
alighting at Camden Town told him he was "no
gentleman". She went away, but directly afterwards, and as the train was starting, reappeared
with her husband, the defendant, who struck complainant with a stick, damaging his hat.

Defendant's wife said the compartment in which
complainant was, appeared to have sufficient
room, so defendant left her to get into it whilst
he found accommodation elsewhere She tried
to open the door but without success, and she
knew that someone was holding it inside. She
tried again, and, as the train had started, she got
on the footboard, and held the dummy handle
by the side of the door Then complainant let
her come in, and as he did so he said the compartment was full. On leaving the train at Camden Town she said she "hoped he would prosper
in his selfishness towards his neighbours". On
being cross-examined she denied saying complainant was no gentleman.

Defendant said his wife was greatly agitated when
she left the train, and told him she had been insulted
by complainant, whereupon he (defendant), as the

2

train was on the move, gave complainant a "tap" on his hat with a stick. The whole thing was done on the "inspiration of the moment".

The stipendiary remarked that nobody had any right to enter a full compartment Those who paid their fare at the starting point, which in this instance was Broad Street, were entitled to a seat, but those who took their tickets at intermediate stations did so subject to there being room for them in the train. Those persons in a carriage which was full had a legal and a moral right to keep the door closed to prevent the carriage being overcrowded, and the sooner the public understood that the better. No one had the right to inconvenience passengers already in their places In this case the complainant was more gallant than he need have been, and his kindness was repaid by defendant's wife making impertinent and sarcastic observations, and then coolly informing her husband that she had been insulted The latter was then moved by an "inspiration" and assaulted the complainant, and now, instead of apologising for his misbehaviour as he ought to have done, he had fought the case to its bitter end Defendant would be fined £5, including costs, or in default be sent to gaol for a month's hard labour.

The following moot point was very recently propounded by the editors of that well-known legal monthly, *Law Notes* :—

" A train arrives at a station; all the carriages of all classes are full. A, having a first class ticket, endeavours to open the door of a first class compartment which already contains its full complement of passengers B objects, and holds the door handle. A insists on endeavouring to enter, and ultimately B thrusts A out of the carriage. A appeals to the stationmaster, who insists on B allowing A to enter."

(i) Has A any remedy against B; or,

(ii) B against A, or,

(iii) A or B against the railway company?

There is really no authoritative decision on all the points raised by the moot, but it appears as to—

(i.) That B acted wrongly when he took the law into his own hands and went so far as to thrust A out, and that consequently A would have a right of action against B for assault and battery. B should not have let A force his way in, or, if he could not prevent this, should have appealed to the stationmaster This case differs somewhat from that of one passenger taking possession of another's seat during the latter's temporary absence, in which event the former occupant of the seat may, it has been held, use reasonable force to expel the intruder as to which see *post*, chapter vii

(ii) B would have no right of action against A because, although the latter acted wrongfully in persisting in entering the compartment, and by so doing rendered himself liable to a £2 penalty, it is only the railway company against whom he has legally trespassed, and they alone could proceed against him for the penalty.

(iii.) There can be little doubt that B would have a right of action against the company in respect of the discomfort and inconvenience caused him by the mismanagement of the stationmaster in allowing A to travel in the full compartment

A curious case was decided early in 1898 by the Correctional Court of Lille (France). An unusually fat man, named Payelle, weighing nearly twenty-five stone, was summoned for contravening the regulations of a railway company Defendant booked third class, but, owing to his abnormal proportions, was unable to enter either a third or second class compartment. He accordingly regaled himself in a first class carriage, and refused to pay the difference in fare, arguing that the company having sold him a third class ticket must find him a seat in a carriage of that description, and that, being unable to get into a third class compartment, he was justified in entering the only carriage the doorway of which was sufficiently wide to admit him. The court, however, upheld the company's contention, which was that if the passenger could not get into a third class carriage he should have taken a ticket entitling him to travel in a carriage of the class into which he could squeeze himself, and that, as only a first class compartment could contain his undue dimensions, he should have booked first class or paid the difference on demand

Judgment was therefore given for the company.

A penalty of £2 is under other bye-laws incurred by passengers wilfully defacing tickets, or riding on any portion of the train not specially set apart for the accommodation of passengers

after request to desist   (It seems a passenger by
riding even on the roof of one of the coaches incurs
no penalty until he has refused to alight after
"request to desist " ')

Possibly some of those passengers who are so
fond of entering or leaving their compartments
whilst the train is in motion are unaware of the
following bye-law :—

" Any passenger entering or leaving, or attempting to enter or leave, any carriage while the train
is in motion, or elsewhere than at the side of the
carriage adjoining the platform or other place
appointed by the company for passengers to alight,
is hereby subjected to a penalty not exceeding
£2 "

It is rarely that this bye-law is put into force
unless the passenger falls or is injured, but it can
be enforced even against a passenger who only
attempts to so enter or leave a train.

In a case heard before Mr Curtis Bennett at
Marylebone Police Court on 14th July, 1899,
defendant was fined £1, with £1 3s costs, for
" that he, being a passenger, unlawfully left the
carriage he was in while it was in motion "   Defendant was a season ticket holder on the line
between Hayes and the City.   Some of the trains
would carry him direct to the City, but sometimes
he would change at Paddington and rush over to
Bishop's Road Station   Defendant said that many
people did the same thing, and he did not see why
he should be singled out.   The stipendiary, in
convicting, remarked that the company had " very

properly taken these proceedings in order to prevent accidents, and to secure the company against litigation initiated by people who disregarded the company's reasonable and proper bye-laws".

One often hears complaints and sees letters in the newspapers regarding the question of passengers smoking in railway carriages and waiting rooms, and I here give the usual bye-law on the subject.—

"Every person smoking in any shed or covered platform of a station, or in any buildings of the company, or in any carriage or compartment of a carriage not specially provided for that purpose, is hereby subjected to a penalty not exceeding £2 The company's officers and servants are required to take the necessary steps to enforce obedience to this bye-law, and any person offending against it is liable, in addition to incurring the penalty above mentioned, to be summarily removed at the first opportunity from the carriage or from the company's premises."

Considering that this bye-law is openly violated by every class of passenger, and at every station throughout the country, it is curious to find the words as to the company's servants being "required to take the necessary steps to enforce obedience," etc., inserted in this bye-law while not appearing in any others

The bye-law is, however, sometimes strictly enforced, and it will be no defence that the offender was sole occupant of the compartment, nor that he had the permission of any other occupant to smoke, nor even that there were no smoking compartments on the train, this being a matter for complaint to the company or Board of Trade, and in no way authorising passengers to break the law An action similar to that maintainable in the case of overcrowding lies against a railway company for allowing smoking in non-smoking carriages or in refreshment or waiting rooms.

It is only the company, however, who can prosecute persons offending against this bye-law, and the same principle applies, as has been said, to the case of a passenger persisting in entering a full compartment, and, indeed, to all other bye-laws

The practice of some individuals who, on entering a compartment containing persons who are complete strangers to them, coolly proceed to light up their pipes, without asking permission or offering any apology, need only be mentioned to be condemned; and it in no way tends to improve matters that the offenders are often persons in a tolerably good position, and who ought to know better.

I suppose there are few people who will object to a fellow passenger smoking provided he has the decency to ask permission, although, as has been pointed out, he remains none the less an offender in the eye of the law

Except in those cases where a break in the journey is permitted (as it always is by implication at an " open " station), a passenger alighting at a station short of the distance the company have contracted to carry him must forfeit all further right to use his ticket, as travellers may not break their journey. This bye-law is not, however, always strictly enforced; and, indeed, seeing that, as has already been pointed out, a passenger cannot legally be made to *give up* his ticket at all, a railway company could take no criminal proceedings against a passenger thus alighting at an intermediate station and refusing to surrender his ticket, provided of course he showed it and gave his name and address if required.

The reasons for this bye-law probably are —

(i.) The risk of a passenger for some purpose of his own returning to his place of departure and fraudulently using the ticket for a second journey, and,

(ii.) That railway companies consider that for every additional advantage the traveller ought to pay.

It has been suggested that both these difficulties might be surmounted by the railway companies requiring travellers to deposit their tickets with some servant of the company during their absence from the station, taking in exchange a receipt for the ticket specifying its date and number, for which a charge of 1d. or 2d. might be made, as in the case of articles left in the cloak room.

The following bye-law is of everyday importance, and requires careful consideration —

"Any passenger using or attempting to use a ticket for any other station than that for which it is available will be required to pay the difference between the sum actually paid and the fare between the stations from and to which the passenger has travelled, or, at the option of the company, the fare from the station to which he was booked to the end of his journey "

Now, if the reader cares to refer to the Regulation of Railways Act, 1889, he will see that passengers proceeding beyond the distance they have booked must pay the "additional fare for the additional distance," and that no option whatever is given railway companies to demand "the difference between the sum actually paid and the fare between the stations from and to which the passenger has travelled".

Two examples will make this point clearer —

(1) The ordinary fare from A to B is 1s., from A to C is 6d, and from B to C 3d. Jones books to B, but, instead of alighting at that station, he goes on to C, there tendering his ticket to B, together with 3d, the fare from B to C. The company, however, decline to accept the money, contending that as Jones, had he in the first instance booked direct to C, would have had to pay 1s 6d., must, as he only booked to B, but has chosen to proceed to C, pay 6d, the difference between the fares from A to B and A to C, which, of course, only makes up the ordinary fare from A to C

Now it is clear, from the wording of the section referred to, that the company's argument is erroneous, and Jones should therefore decline to pay the amount demanded, nor would it make any difference if the company could prove Jones only booked to B with the express object of saving 3d

(11) Suppose the fares from A to B and C are exactly the same, i.e., 1s each, and Jones books to B, but goes on to C, perhaps thinking that the fares being identical he will not be liable to pay anything further. In this belief the passenger will find himself mistaken, as the company will demand, and he will be liable to pay, an additional 3d., i.e., "the additional fare for the additional distance' which he has chosen to travel, namely, from B to C. This point was decided in Pocock's case[1] many years ago

It will thus be apparent that although railway companies "blow hot and cold in the same breath," so to speak, by attempting to extort the "difference between the fares" or the "additional fare for the additional distance," according to whichever best suits them in a pecuniary sense, it is only the latter amount which can be legally recovered, and any other demand should always be strenuously resisted.

Many readers of these lines will no doubt have observed a notice printed on the back of excursion tickets, and now also on all bills announcing such excursions, to the effect that the tickets are only available to and from the stations named upon them, and that any passenger using them on the outward or return journey at any place short of or beyond the said stations will forfeit their tickets and be charged ordinary fare

It has long since been decided that such a con-

dition in the case of excursion or cheap tickets is
binding in so far as it concerns *intermediate* stations
—stations short of the destination mentioned on
the ticket—provided the passenger knew of or had
reasonable means of knowing of the condition
when he purchased his ticket.

But the company's rights in the case of a passenger using an excursion ticket to travel from,
say, London to Chester, and going on in the train
to Rhyl, there giving up his ticket, and tendering
the ordinary fare from Chester to Rhyl, are by no
means clear   The point came up for decision in
1895, in the case of *Palmer v Great Northern Railway
Co*,[1] where Miss Palmer took a cheap ticket from
Peterboro' to Woodhall Spa and back for 4s 6d
The ordinary single fare was 3s. $11\frac{1}{2}$d , and return
7s 11d   The ordinary single fare from Peterboro'
to Horncastle, the next station after leaving
Woodhall Spa, was 4s. $5\frac{1}{2}$d , and return 8s 11d
Miss Palmer went on in the same train to Horncastle, and there tendered the outward half of her
ticket, together with $5\frac{1}{2}$d , the ordinary single fare
from Woodhall Spa to Horncastle, which sum the
collector declined to accept.   On the return
journey Miss Palmer took a $5\frac{1}{2}$d ticket from
Horncastle to Woodhall Spa, which she gave up
with the return half excursion ticket at Peterboro'.
The company sued for the difference between
8s 11d , the ordinary return fare from Peterboro'

---

[1] [1895] 1 Q B 862 , 64 L J Q B , 316 , 72 L T , 287 , 43 W.R.
316 , 11 T , 235

to Horncastle, and 4s. 11½d. actually paid, relying on the following condition printed on the back of the excursion ticket "If used for any other station than that mentioned the ticket will be forfeited, and the full fare must be paid".

The case was first heard in the County Court, where Miss Palmer succeeded, on the ground that the particular condition in question applied only to intermediate stations, and not to stations beyond the terminus mentioned on the ticket

The point being one of considerable importance, leave to appeal was given, on the company's undertaking to pay all costs whatever the result.

The decision of the County Court judge was reversed on appeal, and it was held that the condition was reasonable and binding, and applied not only to intermediate stations but also to stations beyond that to which the company had contracted to carry the passenger.

This decision, however, was always considered to have gone too far, and has since been dissented from (though in an unofficial capacity) by one of the judges who gave it

It will be observed, from what has already been said, that the wording of the condition has since this case undergone a change, it being now expressly extended to stations *beyond* that for which the ticket is issued, and to insure every passenger having notice of the condition it is also printed on all bills announcing excursions.

In a later County Court case, where the facts were identical with those in Palmer's case (the

same railway company, I believe, being concerned
and the ticket being used between the same
stations), an exactly contrary decision was arrived
at, and this in spite of the fact that on the back
of the ticket was printed the new condition to the
effect that the ticket would be forfeited if used for
any station beyond that for which it was issued.
Although, of course, a County Court decision
cannot be taken as in any way overruling one of
the High Court, nevertheless I think that Palmer's
case must now be treated as of practically no
authority whatever first, because on the particular
facts of that case the condition was not broken at
all, as it clearly applied only to intermediate
stations. and secondly, because the condition as
now framed, or as interpreted by the judges in
Palmer's case, is unduly harassing to the public,
and therefore void

It may be asked why if, as already stated, an
ordinary ticket may, by surrendering or showing
it, be used for a station short of the distance contracted for, the same principle should not apply to
an excursion ticket? The answer is that as
railway companies are not required by statute to
issue excursion tickets at all, they are free to
impose more stringent conditions on excursionists
than they can upon ordinary travellers, and when
it is remembered what a large number of day and
half-day trips are now run at extremely low rates,
it would be unfair and very inconvenient to the companies to have passengers alighting at any station
at which the train happened to stop on the journey.

Nevertheless it is submitted that the decision in Palmer's case cannot in any way be supported, for on arrival at Woodhall Spa the contract between the company and Miss Palmer, in so far as concerned the outward journey, expired, the latter, on remaining in the train, being in the position of an ordinary traveller without a ticket, and liable only to pay the ordinary fare from Woodhall Spa to Horncastle, i.e., "the additional fare for the additional distance" Moreover it can hardly be said that the excursion ticket was really "used" to travel with to Horncastle at all; certainly it was given up at that station, but if anything could be said to have been "used" it was the excess fare.

It is difficult to see how railway companies can have any grounds to complain of passengers adopting the course taken by Miss Palmer, for if an excursionist alights at the station named on his ticket, goes away, returns immediately, and books to wherever he wishes to proceed, travelling by the next train, the company could not prevent him doing so, and what possible difference can it make because he chooses to remain in the train?

Also, on the return journey, the company could in no way prevent an excursionist who had travelled beyond the station for which his excursion ticket was issued from re-booking to that station and then continuing in the train

It is usually stated on the bills advertising excursions, and also on the tickets, that the same are available to return on the day of issue, or some

other stated day, or within some specified period,
and by the train named only This is a reasonable condition, and binding on the passenger , and
it follows that if A takes a " week end " ticket—
Friday to Monday—subject to such a condition,
and returns on the Saturday or Sunday, he will be
liable to pay the full ordinary fare, less, perhaps,
the value of the return half ticket

It not at all infrequently happens that a passenger uses his ticket for a superior class The
following is the bye-law on the subject —

" Any person travelling without the special permission of some duly authorised servant of the
company in a carriage or by a train of superior
class to that for which his ticket is issued is
hereby subjected to. a penalty not exceeding £2,
and shall in addition be liable to pay the fare
according to the class of carriage in which he is
travelling from the station whence the train originally started, unless he shows that he had no
intention to defraud "

With regard to the latter part of the bye-law—
about paying the fare from the station from
which the train started—it may as well be disposed of at once by saying that it is unreasonable
and void

Of course it will be obvious that the mere fact
of a passenger travelling in a superior class of
carriage is not *per se* any evidence of intent to
defraud, and to secure a conviction the onus lies
on the company to show by means of evidence
(circumstantial or otherwise) that the passenger

had such an intention. Perhaps this subject will be best exemplified by some examples:—

(1) Smith has a third class ordinary or season ticket, and although there is ample third class room he nevertheless rides in a second class compartment If, on completing his journey, Smith leaves the station simply giving up his ticket, or saying "season," or nothing at all, and does not state that he has travelled second class, nor offer any explanation, this would be *primâ facie* evidence of fraud, and Smith, if prosecuted, might experience considerable difficulty in rebutting this presumption Of course he might plead that having met with a friend who had a second class ticket he had travelled with him, quite intending to pay the excess fare, but the matter had slipped his memory at the last moment

Possibly this might be the true explanation, and it would rest with the justices to decide from the surrounding circumstances whether or not defendant was to be believed; and, indeed, if the company could offer no further evidence, the case would doubtless be dismissed.

On the other hand, the company might make sure of a conviction by adducing evidence to prove defendant had travelled in superior class under the like circumstances on other occasions without paying the difference in fare, which would be almost conclusive against him. But even this might not be so, and, in order to show how a criminal intention may sometimes be explained away, I would draw the reader's attention to a

curious case, decided a few years ago, where a
man who was summoned for riding without a
ticket with intent to defraud on several specified
dates, pleaded, in answer to the charge, that he
formerly had a season ticket, and got so accustomed to the call for tickets, and the habit of
taking no notice of it unless season tickets were
specially asked for, that on some occasions he had
forgotten to show his ticket, and at other times
the collector had passed the door without so much
as asking him for it, thinking he was still a season
ticket holder   As defendant was able to substan-
tiate his plea by producing a number of old tickets
the charge against him was dismissed

But to return to the bye-law under consideration and suppose—

(ii) That the third class compartments were
full, or even most of them full (for passengers
cannot always be expected to run all over the
train to seek room), there would be no evidence of
any intention on Smith's part to defraud the company although he said nothing on handing his
ticket to the collector.

(iii) If, as is often the case, tickets are examined
at a ticket platform whilst the passengers remain
in the train, the mere fact of Smith simply giving
up a third class ticket and offering no explanation
would not, apart from other circumstances, be any
evidence of fraud, as he acts openly, and the ticket
collector will observe what class of carriage the
passenger is riding in, if he declines to pay the
excess fare, the company's only remedy will be

to take his name and address and sue for the amount

Cases must naturally now and then arise where both ordinary and season ticket holders travel for some special reason in a superior class notwithstanding there may be room in the inferior, *e g* , there may be no smoking compartments of the inferior class on the train, and the passenger may desire to smoke In such instances the safer course is to point out the fact on collection of tickets, which will obviate the possible risk of criminal proceedings, and, indeed, if there is any reasonable excuse for travelling in the superior class, the company will rarely sue for the excess fare.

In a case where a passenger travelled second class as a protest against there being no cushions in the thirds, and the company prosecuted him, the stipendiary held that although the passenger simply gave up his third class ticket without comment yet there was not sufficient evidence of fraudulent design to justify a conviction.

Those foolish persons who cut the window straps, or in any way do wilful damage to the company's property, are liable to heavy penalties, the usual bye-law providing that . " Any person who wilfully cuts or tears any lining or window strap, or curtains, removes or defaces any number plate, or breaks or scratches any window of a carriage used on the railway, or who otherwise, except by unavoidable accident, damages, defaces or injures any such carriage or any station or other property of the company, is hereby subjected to a penalty not exceeding £5, in addition to the amount of any damage for which he may be liable "

Supposing, however, a passenger accidentally breaks a window, or, without negligence, otherwise unintentionally damages the company's property, he is neither liable to any penalty nor can he be successfully sued in respect of the injury done, no one being answerable for a pure accident, but if the damage was in any way attributable to the passenger's negligence or misconduct it would not be purely accidental, and he would be liable.

Examples —

(i) A slips on entering a compartment, and breaks the window with his umbrella. A is not liable

(ii) A is carelessly swinging his stick about, and in so doing smashes a window A is responsible because of his negligence

(iii) A breaks the window whilst wrongfully assaulting B A is liable because of his misconduct.

When a window is broken, a demand for 7s 6d, the cost of repairing it, is usually made by some servant of the company Under these circumstances, provided the breakage is *purely accidental*, the passenger should decline to pay, but give his name and address instead, when he will probably hear no more of the matter, but if the breakage was not wholly accidental the passenger had better pay and obtain a receipt as soon as possible, and think himself lucky if he escapes a prosecution for doing wilful damage under the above-mentioned bye-law.

In a case heard by one of the Metropolitan magistrates in November, 1899, defendant had an appointment at the War Office of an urgent nature. On arriving at the station, just before the departure of the train, he found all the carriages full. He attempted to enter a first class compartment, but the occupants held the door from the inside to prevent him doing so. Thereupon he proceeded to vindicate his grievance against the railway company by smashing the window with his walking stick. Afterwards he repented of this act of destruction, and wrote a letter of apology to the company offering to pay for the injury done.

Notwithstanding this, the company prosecuted him for doing wilful damage; the stipendiary, however, taking the view that they had acted in a very high-handed manner, considering the circumstances inflicted only a nominal penalty of 3d., assessed the damage at the same amount, and allowed no costs. But this decision must not be taken as any authority whatever for passengers to break windows, however much they may be exasperated by a railway company's persistent mismanagement.

No doubt a great deal of disease is spread by persons suffering from infectious disorders travelling about in defiance of the following very proper bye-law providing that—

"The company may refuse to carry any person who has any infectious disorder. If any person who has any such disorder is found upon the premises of the company, or travels or attempts to travel upon the railway of the company without the special permission of the company, he shall be liable to a penalty not exceeding £2, in addition to the forfeiture of any fare which he may have paid, and may be removed at the first opportunity from the company's premises. Any person who has charge of any person suffering from an infectious disorder while upon the premises of the company, or travelling or attempting to travel upon the railway, or who aids or assists any person suffering from such disorder in being upon the premises of the company, or travelling or attempting to travel on the railway, shall be liable to a penalty not exceeding £2, unless the person so suffering from the disorder be travelling by the special permission of the company "

Any person taking or sending loaded firearms by train, or *bringing the same* upon any part of a railway company's premises, is liable to a penalty of £5

Persons in a state of intoxication, using foul or abusive language, or writing obscene or offensive words on any part of the company's stations or carriages, or committing any nuisance, or in any way wilfully interfering with the comfort of other passengers, are liable to a £2 fine, and may be removed from the company's premises.

Dogs (except ladies' lap dogs) and other animals are not strictly allowed to accompany passengers into the carriages Dogs should be muzzled and put into the van or other place provided for their accommodation. A penalty of £2 may be inflicted for infringement of this bye-law The usual fare must be paid for the carriage of these animals according to a fixed scale

In Belgium, however, dogs are treated with the respect due to the canine race, and travel as passengers

In a case decided not long ago by a Belgian Court, the facts were that a hunting man took a ticket for his retriever, and the faithful animal sat beside his master On the train becoming rather crowded the dog was unceremoniously turned off his seat by the guard to make room for a passenger, and had to crouch down beneath the legs of the human occupants of the carriage It was held that a dog is as much entitled to a seat as his master, and, consequently, that when a compartment has room for ten passengers, and there are five men and five dogs therein, it must be considered as full

Besides the pecuniary and other penalties provided for the prevention of offences against their bye-laws, railway companies also possess the right, which they freely exercise, of publishing the full names and addresses, with particulars as to the punishments meted out to those persons convicted under such bye-laws

These interesting announcements are usually made periodically—about three months or so after committal of the offence, and when people have begun to forget all about it—by means of what has appropriately been termed the "railway pillory," consisting of a placard headed, "Caution List of Convictions," after which follow, in tabular form, the offenders' full names and addresses, the dates and nature of the offences, and the penalties imposed

Some companies, instead of printing these long lists, select a few offenders, whose names they print on separate bills, with the full details in very large type and red ink, which plan is, of course, far worse for the individuals selected

The notices, whatever form they take, are invariably posted up at all the company's stations in the district.

The person whose conviction is thus emblazoned abroad has no right to sue the company for damages for libel, as, provided the statement is true, that will be an absolute bar to civil proceedings, the law not deeming it right that a man should be considered to have any better character than he in fact possesses, and that he can have suffered no legal wrong by the truth being known And even though it could be proved that a person's name was published simply in order to ruin him, and for no other purpose whatever, this would, nevertheless, give him no right to recover any compensation It would be different, however, were the statement in any material particular false, e g., saying the imprisonment was "with hard labour," such not being the case.

A plea of truth alone is no bar to criminal proceedings for libel, but as it could be validly pleaded that the statement was made for the public benefit, and as a warning to others, no such proceedings could be successfully carried through.

On some persons, however, even this publication of their names seems to have no effect. In a recent case, where a woman was fined for travelling without paying her fare with intent to defraud the company, it was stated she had already been convicted nineteen times for similar offences both in her own name and under various *aliases*.

In conclusion of this chapter it may be added that statute law provides that if the infraction or non-observance of the company's bye-laws be attended with danger or annoyance to the public or hindrance to the company in the lawful use of the railway, the company may summarily interfere to obviate or remove such danger, annoyance or hindrance, and that without prejudice to any penalty incurred by the infraction of any such bye-law

By an earlier Act it is also provided that if any person wilfully obstructs or injures any officer or agent of the company in the execution of his duty, the person offending, and all persons assisting him, may be seized and detained until they can conveniently be taken before a justice, and shall, in the discretion of such justice, forfeit any sum not exceeding £5, and in default of payment be imprisoned for any term not exceeding two months.

CHAPTER II.

On the granting of a season ticket the company enters into a contract with the passenger, undertaking, in consideration of a lump sum paid in advance, to carry him as often as he likes during the period stated on the ticket, by any of their ordinary trains running between the stations and by the routes therein named.

Season tickets, like those of the ordinary kind, must be produced for inspection whenever required by any authorised servant of the company. But this does not mean that a season ticket holder is to be obliged to produce his ticket at the mere whim or fancy of some disagreeable or officious inspector or porter, *e.g* , if a ticket collector informs a passenger that he intends to examine the latter's season ticket "every time," although not asking for those of other persons, the passenger would be justified in declining to produce the ticket, and should offer his name and address, and complain to headquarters of the collector's vexatious conduct.

It must be remembered that whilst railway companies are bound to issue ordinary tickets to all persons who are in a fit state to travel and tender the fare, they cannot be compelled either to issue or renew season tickets

The reason for this distinction is that, as has already been said, a season ticket is a contract, and nobody can be forced to enter into any contract except by the authority of Parliament. Nor would it make the slightest difference, even assuming the ticket to be refused owing to a mere personal grudge on the part of some director or superintendent of the company; for, having a legal right to refuse to enter into a contract, the court would not investigate the motives for such refusal In fact the same principle applies as in the case of Jones opening a shop next door to Smith's shop already established, not for the purpose of trade but avowedly to ruin Smith by underselling him, and for which injury the latter could obtain no redress.

The conditions providing penalties and forfeiture of the ticket on lending or transferring, or attempting to lend or transfer, it to any other person are perfectly valid It would appear also that if there is (as is usually the case) a condition on the ticket to the effect that same is only available for the journey when produced to any officer of the company on demand, a passenger who had forgotten to bring his ticket with him could be successfully sued for the ordinary fare notwithstanding he gave his name and address, and could prove that the ticket was in force when he was called upon to produce it. There is some doubt, however, as to the validity of this condition, and the railway companies, be it said to their credit, do not often attempt to strictly enforce it, provided the passenger gives his name and address in case he has not got his ticket with him.

But travellers should be careful always to carry their season tickets, and thus save themselves and the railway company trouble and annoyance

It has been decided that a stipulation contained in the form of conditions on which season tickets are granted to the public, providing that if the holder loses his ticket, or fails to surrender it on the very day following that on which it expires, the deposit paid on the issue of the ticket will be forfeited, is valid.

In July, 1899, the Great Northern Railway Company sued to recover damages, which they estimated at £5, from a City clerk, for having failed to return his expired season ticket The company's solicitor appeared to support the case, which was heard in Bloomsbury County Court by His Honour Judge Bacon

Defendant explained that the season ticket was not renewed at the time because he contemplated changing his address. The ticket had been mislaid or lost

The solicitor said there was no imputation against defendant's honesty, but a vast amount of trouble had been caused by the non-return of the ticket.

The judge having asked what was the value of the ticket, the solicitor replied that it was worth a shilling.

His Honour, in giving judgment for the company for 1s *and costs,* said that although, possibly, as the solicitor had suggested, the ticket might be found and used by some fraudulent person, yet he could not assess the damages on that basis, and that any damages the company might sustain beyond the 1s. would be too remote to be recoverable.

It is doubtful if this decision would apply to the case of an ordinary passenger losing his ticket or failing to surrender it, for the reason that whilst season ticket holders are expressly required by their contract with the company to return their tickets at the end of the period for which the same are issued, there is no legal obligation to give up an ordinary ticket at all.

A season ticket must, of course, be used by the route specified only, anyone using it by another route without the permission of an officer of the company, and simply saying "season" when asked for his ticket, runs the risk of a conviction for fraud, unless, indeed, the ticket had been ordered for the other route, or it was a recognised thing for season ticket holders to travel by such route

In any case, if the passenger points out that he is travelling by a different route to that mentioned in his contract, the company's only remedy is to sue for the fare.

In this country it is unusual for trade advertisements to be printed on the backs of season tickets, but such appears to be the custom in France, where a barrister recently sued the French Western

Railway Company, contesting their right to print advertisements on his ticket.

The company counterclaimed against plaintiff for instituting frivolous and vexatious proceedings; but, nevertheless, the court decided in his favour, on the ground, apparently, that he had not contracted to become a "walking advertisement," and, moreover, that such announcements were the result of independent contracts between the company and other persons in which the passenger had no interest

CHAPTER III.

UNPUNCTUALITY OF TRAINS, ETC

THE following is an extract from the "General Regulations" of the London and North-Western Railway Company —

"The published time-tables of this company are only intended to fix the time at which passengers may be certain to obtain their tickets for any journey from the various stations, it being understood that the trains shall not depart before the appointed times. The directors give notice that the company do not undertake that the trains shall start or arrive at the times specified in the bills; nor will they be accountable for any loss, inconvenience or injury which may arise from delays or detention The right to stop the trains at any station on the line, though not marked as a stopping station, is reserved."

The unpunctuality of trains and consequent missing of connections, so persistently occurring at some junctions, is one of the railway traveller's chief grievances. Notwithstanding the above regulation, if the company advertises a train to arrive or depart at a certain time, and, owing to their or their servants' negligence, a delay occurs whereby a passenger suffers loss, he may recover damages from the company.

But railway companies usually also have a condition providing that they will not be responsible
for any delays, etc., except such as arise from the
wilful neglect or default of themselves or their
servants. This condition has been held to be
reasonable; and, in order to succeed in any action
he may bring against a railway company, the
passenger would have to furnish proof of such
misconduct

The reader will, doubtless, ask, "What would
amount to 'wilful neglect or default'?" This is
a somewhat difficult question upon which to lay
down any general rule, and is, indeed, one for the
jury to decide after considering the facts of each
individual case The following may, however, be
taken as examples of such 'wilful neglect or
default' —

(i) A train is unable to proceed owing to the
engine-driver having omitted to take a sufficient
supply of water before starting.

(ii) A signalman allows a slow goods train to
proceed in front of a passenger train then nearly
due, well knowing that the result of his so doing
must be to cause a delay

(iii) A train arrives at a junction where it has,
say, five minutes to wait, there is a horsebox
attached to the train which has to be taken off,
but the company's servants take no steps to shunt
off the horsebox till the train is due to depart, thus
causing a delay

In order to render a railway company liable
because a train is late the onus usually rests on

the plaintiff to prove the delay was occasioned by the company's or their servants' negligence. However, the extreme or persistent lateness of a train would raise the presumption of negligence, which presumption it would be open to the company to rebut by showing that the delay was due to something beyond their control, *e g*, fog, floods or snowdrift

In *Woodgate v Great Western Railway Co.*,[1] plaintiff, on Christmas Eve, 1881, took a first class ticket from Paddington to Bridgnorth On the return half of his ticket were printed the words " see back," and on the outward half the words "issued subject to the conditions stated in the company's time tables" On the first page of the time tables was a notice headed "train bills," to the effect that the company would not be responsible for any injury arising from delays unless occasioned by their servants' wilful misconduct. Owing to the holiday season, foggy weather, and to a collision which had occurred a few hours previously, the plaintiff's journey was scarcely as expeditious as might have been desired, Mr. Woodgate not reaching Bridgnorth till four hours after the time appointed.

In the action which he subsequently brought against the company, it was held—

(i) That the conditions in the time bills were incorporated into the plaintiff's contract with the company ; and,

---

[1] [1884] 51 *L. T.*, 826 , 33 *W R.*, 428

(11) That as there was no evidence of the company's or their servants' wilful misconduct, the action must fail.

Smith, J, said· "The taking of the ticket, the time table and the conditions, formed the contract under which the Great Western Railway Co. undertook to carry Mr Woodgate. Then . . the question arises, what is the meaning of the contract? I think no man can read this clause without coming to one conclusion It does not say 'we will be liable in no case,' but it simply says this, 'if you, as a passenger, have sustained any loss, inconvenience or injury, by reason of delay or detention, we will compensate you if you prove it is by the wilful misconduct of our servants, but otherwise not '."

By booking a passenger the company impliedly contract to carry him to his destination with all reasonable despatch; and if, through missing a connection, the traveller would be delayed for an unreasonable length of time (depending on the circumstances of the case, a point for the jury to decide) he would be entitled to charge the company with any costs properly incurred in completing it in some other manner (e.g, by taking a cab) and any incidental expenses. If there were no other train at a reasonable hour the same day, hotel expenses, according to the passenger's station in life, could be recovered. But any such expenses must be the natural and reasonable consequence of the company's negligent delay, so, where a man stayed three days at an hotel awaiting the arrival of a parcel delayed by the company's negligence, it was decided that he was not entitled to his expenses

It seems that some railway companies have instructed their booking clerks to refuse in certain cases to issue through tickets to any passengers who will have to change trains at some junction in order to reach their destinations, unless there is either a margin of ten minutes or more between the arrival of the one train and the departure of the other at the junction, or there is a later train from the junction the same day calling at the station to which the traveller wants to go.

This is obviously done with a view to relieve the company from liability in case the train misses the connection. So long, however, as the company continue to show the connection in their time tables, and state the fare on their table of fares, they cannot legally refuse a ticket to anyone tendering the amount thereof, unless, perhaps, they have before given him express notice that they refuse to book him beyond the junction by that particular train, and that the connection as shown on the time table is withdrawn

Although a passenger cannot recover damages on account of mere annoyance or disappointment, yet he may do so in respect of *personal inconvenience*, provided it is of a substantial nature; but it does not necessarily follow that he can recover for all consequences, however remotely following from the detention and inconvenience.

In an instructive case on this subject,[1] decided in 1875, it appears that a family booked from Wimbledon to Hampton Court by the last train at night Instead of going to Hampton Court, however, as stated in the company's time table, the train went to Esher, at which village neither accommodation for the night nor any conveyance was to be had Consequently, although it was a dark and wet night, the party had to walk home, arriving at 3 A.M , and, as one of the results, the wife caught cold and was ill for a long time, and unable to assist her husband in his business.

It was held that the husband and wife were entitled to damages for the inconvenience suffered owing to being obliged to walk home, but *not for the illness* and its consequences, on the ground that any such damage was too remote to be recoverable, it not being (so said the Court) the natural result of the company's default for the lady to catch cold by walking a few miles on a rainy night.

As has been said, a traveller may in certain cases be justified in taking a cab and charging the cost thereof to the defaulting company; but he must not do so unreasonably or vexatiously, as, *e.g.*, where the delay is only slight, or where he would not complete his journey appreciably quicker by so doing than by proceeding by the next train

In some rare instances a passenger may even be

---

[1] *Hobbs v L & S.W Railway Co*, 10 Q B , 111 , 44 L.J Q B. 49 , 32 L T., 352 , 23 W R , 530.

justified in taking a special train owing to missing a connection. It should be remembered, however, that a special train is an expensive luxury, and hardly worth indulging in unless one is practically certain of being able to look to the company for the cost Before, therefore, anyone takes a special train, with the intention of afterwards suing the company, he should first ask himself two questions, namely :—

(i.) "Is my business of such importance that, supposing I had missed the connection through no fault of the company, I should, at my own expense, have ordered a special train ?" and, if so,

(ii.) "Have I a reasonable prospect of being able to prove this in a court of law ? '

If the traveller can conscientiously answer both these questions in the affirmative, let him take his special train, otherwise not

On this matter the case of *Le Blanche* v. *London and North-Western Railway Co.*[1] may be referred to as a suitable example. Plaintiff booked first class from Liverpool to Scarborough, per London and North-Western Railway, by the 2 P M train, which, according to the time tables, was due at Scarborough at 7.30 P M   Mr. Le Blanche had to change trains both at Leeds and York, and in each case to enter a train *not* belonging to the London and North - Western Company. The North-Western train arrived twenty-seven min-

---

[1] [1876] 1 *C P D*, 286, 45 *L J C.P.*, 521, 34 *L T*, 667, 24 *W R*, 808.

utes late at Leeds, in consequence whereof plaintiff
missed his connection, thus not reaching York till
7 P.M., too late for the train on to Scarborough   The
next train was due to leave York at 8 P M., and
reach Scarborough at 10 P M., and on hearing this
Mr Le Blanche immediately ordered a special train
and arrived at his destination at 8 30 P M.   The
train cost plaintiff nearly £12, and he subsequently
sued the London and North-Western Railway Company to recover the sum he had paid

It was held that notwithstanding the delay was
clearly attributable to that company's negligence,
yet Mr Le Blanche could not succeed in his claim,
because although if the party bound to perform a
contract fails in his duty the other party may
perform it for him, and charge him the reasonable
expense incurred in so doing, yet he must not act
in an unreasonable or vexatious manner, and that
it was absurd for anyone to take a special train
simply to reach a pleasant place an hour and a
half earlier

It follows from this decision that a person having
a business appointment to keep may under certain
circumstances take a special train in order to enable him to fulfil his engagement, and charge the
expense to the company, but only if he could prove
that he would have done so at his own cost had
he known that he could not recover the expense
from anyone else.   In general, however, no compensation can be recovered on account of the loss
of business or other engagements through the
lateness of trains, the law considering any such

damages as being too remote a consequence of the company's default, or, in other words, that the probability of such a loss occurring could not have been in the contemplation of both parties at the time of entering into the contract; and, more-over, seeing that railway companies have no option as regards the issuing of ordinary tickets to pas-sengers tendering the fare, it would make no difference although the traveller, on taking his ticket, told the clerk of some particular loss he (the passenger) would sustain in case the train were late.

Suppose, however, a train is professedly run for a special purpose, for which purpose the company must be presumed to know that passengers have purchased their tickets, the case would be different Thus, where a miller, who had taken a ticket to attend the Mark Lane corn market by special train run on the particular day, missed his market owing to the train being late, he recovered £10 damages; and, in another case, a miner got a day's wages, lost through an unreasonable delay in starting a train.

As all travellers will be aware, railway companies are accustomed to make certain monthly altera-tions in their train services, the principal of which come into operation in May, July and October Adequate notice of such alterations must be given, and any failure in this respect on the company's part may render them liable to pay heavy dam-ages For example, suppose that, without giving due notice thereof, a railway company discontinue a train, or run it ten minutes earlier, whereby an intending passenger is delayed and inconvenienced, he would have the right to recover any damages naturally resulting from the company's carelessness.

While it is thus the company's duty to give sufficient notice of any changes, it is at the same time incumbent on passengers to acquaint themselves with the time tables, and not to assume that the trains will continue the same from month to month; and, indeed, it sometimes happens that an important item is accidentally omitted from the bills announcing the alterations

Railway companies are not, strictly speaking, bound to issue time tables at all, but, as they do issue them, the same amount to an offer and contract to carry, and are a representation that not only their own trains but also the trains of other companies will, *if shown on the time table*, run in conformity therewith.

If time tables are expressed to be issued for a certain period (say for May and June) the contract expires at the end of the time mentioned, and probably in such a case no action would lie against the company for loss sustained by reason of the alteration of a train, even assuming no notice whatever had been given thereof, and that the loss occurred on the first day of the month in which the alteration took effect—the passenger thus having very possibly had no reasonable opportunity of seeing the new time tables.

If, however, a time table is stated to be for

certain period " and until further notice," the company must give due warning of any intended change, and a traveller who had not had a reasonable chance of ascertaining that the old time table was cancelled by the new one could successfully sue the company for any loss sustained

In case an advertised train is *not in fact run at all,* or not run on some particular occasion, an action will lie at the suit of any intending passenger, unless the non-running of the train was due to some circumstance altogether beyond the company's control, or proper notice had been given of the discontinuance. Thus in *Denton* v *Great Northern Railway Co,*[1] plaintiff, an engineer, had to go from Peterborough to Hull, where he had an appointment for the next morning. From the defendant company's time tables it appeared that a train left Peterborough at 7 P.M , reaching Hull about midnight. On arrival at Milford Junction Mr. Denton found that the train to Hull had been discontinued, and that he could not get there that night. The line from Milford to Hull belonged to the North Eastern Railway Co., who till 1st March had run a train departing a few minutes after arrival of the 7 P.M. from Peterborough, and, although the Great Northern Railway Co. had received notice of the discontinuance, they nevertheless continued to show the connection in their time tables. Owing to this misrepresentation Mr. Denton did not reach Hull in time for his appoint-

[1] [1856] 5 *E & B*, 860, 25 *L.J Q B*, 129

ment, and suffered loss to the extent of £5 10s., for which amount he successfully sued the railway company. In giving judgment, Lord Campbell said. "It is all one as if a person duly authorised by the company, had, knowing it was not true, said to the plaintiff, 'There is a train from Milford to Hull at that hour'. The plaintiff believes this, acts upon it, and sustains loss. It is well established law that where a person makes an untrue statement, knowing it to be untrue, to another, who is induced to act upon it, an action lies. The facts bring the present case within that rule."

Some railway companies make it a practice not to give notice of the cessation of the issue of their summer weekly cheap tickets till about the very day before the discontinuance. Such notice as this is utterly inadequate, and any intending traveller could demand a ticket at the cheap rate, and, in case of refusal, recover from the company the excess sum paid in order to travel at the ordinary fare

Not long ago a Leicester gentleman and his wife recovered damages from the London and North-Western Railway Company under the following circumstances: In November, 1898, the company advertised "long date" excursion tickets to Edinburgh at a single fare for the double journey On 6th December plaintiffs obtained a bill with this offer thereon, and three days later applied for tickets They were then informed that the offer had been withdrawn and a new one substituted applying to merely "short date" facilities. Plaintiffs subsequently sued for £2 10s., the difference between the advertised price of the "long date" excursion tickets and two ordinary return tickets to Edinburgh. The judge held that the company had failed to give reasonable notice of the withdrawal of the "long date" offer, and gave plaintiffs judgment for £2 6s., with costs.

Suppose Smith, coming straight from France, refers to a railway company's time table, and acts on a statement therein contained to the effect that a train for a particular place starts from, say, Euston at a fixed time. On reaching the station he finds that, owing to a strike or for some other reason, the train has been discontinued after issue of the time table to which he referred. Notice of such discontinuance was given by public advertisement. Smith, however, avers he knew nothing, and had no opportunity of knowing anything, about the discontinuance of the train, and brings an action against the company for damages. Will he succeed? This is at present a moot point, but it is submitted, on the general principles of law governing the branch of contract and of offer and acceptance, that as the company's time tables amount in law to an offer to carry, passengers are at liberty to treat such offer as still subsisting, and open for their acceptance, so long as they have not, directly or indirectly, received any notice of its withdrawal, and that consequently Smith could recover compensation.

On bank holidays all railway companies give notice that certain specified trains (chiefly such as are used by persons going to and returning from business) will not be run. This custom has now become so prevalent that passengers would probably, in many instances, be deemed to have notice of the discontinuance; but, it seems clear, although there is little authority on the point, that supposing a traveller to be able to prove that he had not in any way received actual or constructive notice that the train would not be run, he could successfully sue the company.

A passenger may recover any damages incurred owing to his being put into a wrong train by one of the company's servants, or if the company or their servants so act as to bring a passenger to suppose the train was going in the direction in which he was desirous of travelling, *e.g*, Brown is in the habit of travelling frequently from Crewe to Preston by a certain train from a particular platform, and one day the company, without taking special precautions to obviate the risk of regular passengers being misled, start a train for Chester from the accustomed platform, and at about the usual departure time of Brown's train, and by which the latter travels, mistaking it for the usual train to Preston. Here Brown would have a good cause of action against the company, who could not plead contributory negligence on the passenger's part in making no inquiry as to where the train was going, as it would be unreasonable to expect him to do so—he being a regular traveller. If, however, Brown was not a regular passenger, the company would, no doubt, succeed in resisting his claim on the ground aforesaid.

Further, suppose passengers are accustomed to their trains starting from a particular platform, it will be the company's duty, on making any alteration in the starting place, to see that no passengers are left on the wrong platform, or in the refreshment rooms, etc, awaiting the arrival of the train, and any failure in this duty will render the company liable in damages.

It sometimes happens, particularly at intermediate stations on a main line, that an express train stops alongside the platform, owing to some signal check, at about the same time as a local train, going in the same direction, is due to arrive Under such circumstances a passenger often mistakes the express for the local train, and occasionally gets carried a good deal farther than he contracted for or desired. Now, notwithstanding that the company will have thus taken him a considerable distance for his money, and will have to bring him back free of cost, this will, perhaps, be poor solace to the passenger if he has suffered much loss by the delay, and he will be anxious to know whether he is entitled to any recompense from the company.

Apart from other circumstances, the mere stopping of the express at an intermediate station would not *per se* be a sufficient invitation to passengers to enter the train, but supposing a porter had previously told the passenger that his train would be "next in," the latter would be guilty of no contributory negligence in entering the next train that arrived, and so could recover damages from the company

The like principles apply to trains which are divided *en route*, *e g*, front part goes to Liverpool, back part to Birmingham, and while a traveller getting into the wrong portion without making any inquiry would be debarred by his carelessness from successfully suing the company, it is at the same time the latter's duty to take reasonable precautions to prevent passengers being misled, and neglect to do so would render the company answerable in damages.

If, owing to a traveller being conveyed by a wrong train, it subsequently becomes futile for him to proceed to his intended destination, he could recover the fare paid, on the ground of total failure of the consideration.

In case a passenger is carried beyond his proper station, owing to the carriage door being locked or sticking fast, he is entitled to be refunded any out-of-pocket expenses properly incurred owing to the delay (*e.g.*, cab fare, cost of a meal or hotel expenses), in some cases also to damages, and, in rare instances, to the cost of a special train, as to which see *ante*, p 52.

CHAPTER IV.

LUGGAGE

(a) "Personal" Luggage

All passengers have the right to take with them on their journeys, free of cost, a certain amount of personal luggage.

This right is secured by clauses in the various Acts of Parliament incorporating each company. The usual amount allowed free is now 150 lb for each first class passenger, 120 lb. for each second class passenger, and 100 lb. for each third class passenger.

From one case it seems that if each traveller is allowed 60 lb of luggage free, a man and wife may carry 120 lb. between them, although the bulk of it is the husband's

Luggage exceeding the specified weight, or other than "ordinary" or "personal" luggage, must be paid for according to fixed rates. As to excess luggage, the railway companies have recently issued notices to the effect that in future they will rigidly enforce their rights with regard thereto, the carriage to be paid in advance at the starting point.

A passenger by excursion train—" no luggage allowed "—must, if he takes luggage, pay for the whole amount.

(62)

As to the meaning of the words "ordinary" or "personal" luggage—though at first sight one might think it was an easy matter to determine—it is by no means so plain. From a perusal of numerous (some of them very contradictory) decisions, it may be said that it comprises the traveller's clothing, and such things as are needful for his personal use and convenience, according to the habits of his class.

Clothing, then, it is clear, a traveller may take with him as personal luggage, but what else he may carry for his "personal use and convenience" is very uncertain, and it is easier to enumerate the things he may not take

Of course merchandise and articles to be sold at a profit may not be taken, but many people will be surprised to hear that the following things also have (*inter alia*) been excluded from the designation of personal luggage :—

(i.) An artist's sketches.[1]

(ii.) A child's rocking-horse.[2]

(iii.) The papers of a solicitor [3]

(iv) Some sheets, blankets and quilts which a man returning from abroad brought with him

---

[1] *Mytton* v *M. Railway Co* [1859], 4 *H. & N*, 615, 28 *L J Ex*, 398

[2] *Hudston* v *M Railway Co* [1869], 4 *Q B*, 366; 38 *L J Q B* 213; 20 *L.T*, 526

[3] *Phelps* v *L & N W. Railway Co.* [1865], 19 *C.B.* (N S), 321, 34 *L.J C P.*, 259, 12 *L T*, 496, 13 *W R.*, 782, 11 *Jur* (N S.), 652.

with the intention of permanently settling down in a certain part of England.[1]

Some years ago a County Court judge decided that a hamper of fowls, fruit and vegetables, intended as a present for a friend, came within the definition of personal luggage; but this decision is inconsistent with the authorities.

Railway companies are responsible as insurers for all luggage if carried in the van; and, in the absence of contributory negligence on the passenger's part, they are liable to the same extent for luggage which the traveller takes with him into his compartment. The company are *not answerable at all* for anything not being personal luggage which a passenger causes to be conveyed as if it were such; but the company will be liable if, well knowing that the luggage is not what it purports to be, they, nevertheless, carry it as if it were, without objection.

On a traveller reaching his destination, it is the company's duty to have the luggage ready for delivery at the proper place, and their liability as insurers continues during the transit of the luggage from train to cab and *vice versa* The traveller cannot, however, make the company's responsibility continue for an unreasonable time after leaving the train, except, perhaps, as warehousemen.

It should be borne in mind that if a passenger

---

[1] *Macrow v G W Railway* [1871], 6 Q.B., 712, 40 L.J.Q.B., 300, 24 L T., 618

has an opportunity of taking his luggage away, but, instead of so doing, consigns it to a porter to take charge of for a time, there will have been in effect a delivery of the luggage to the passenger and a re-delivery by the latter to the porter as the *traveller's agent*, and not as servant of the company, who, consequently, will be exempt from liability if it is lost.

From a case[1] decided in 1884 it appears that a porter, on a lady arriving at Ashton-under-Lyne Station, took her luggage from the van and asked her if she would have a cab, and so take it with her. She, however, said she would walk, and send for the luggage afterwards. Thereupon the porter undertook to put it aside and keep it for her. Two hours later the luggage was sent for, but it was nowhere to be found. It was held that the company were not liable for the loss, as the luggage had been duly delivered in the ordinary way, and the re-delivery to the porter could not be taken to affect them. Possibly the porter might be liable for the loss if it could be shown that it was attributable to his gross negligence. But the case would have been differently decided had the plaintiff been offered no opportunity of taking possession of her belongings.

Persons *about to go* by train should also be careful how they act in handing their luggage to porters. In one case an intending passenger for

---

[1] *Hodkinson* v *L. & N.W. Railway Co*, 14 Q.B.D., 228, 32 W.R., 662.

Hull, on arriving in a cab at a Manchester station, without giving any instructions as to his destination, handed his bag to a porter, which the latter left on the platform. The passenger afterwards found it there, and, being unable to get another porter, labelled it himself. He then went away for a few minutes, and on his return the property had disappeared. The company were held not liable for the loss. Supposing, however, the traveller, when handing his luggage to the porter, had stated where he was going, and asked that the luggage should be labelled, or if he had simply said " Hull," the case would have been different,[1] the luggage being thenceforward in the company's custody as common carriers, and a notice that " the company's servants are forbidden to take charge of any article," and that " any articles which a passenger wishes to leave at a station should be deposited in the cloak room," would not avail to free the company from liability.

In another case[2] a passenger missed his train, and handed his luggage to a porter to keep for him till the next train, which was not due for an hour.

The traveller then left the station and went to the billiard room of an hotel, but on his return the luggage was missing. It was held that the porter took charge of the luggage solely on his own responsibility, and that the company were not answerable for the loss.

[1] *Lovell v L C & D. Railway* [1876], 45 L J Q B , 476, 34 L T , 127 , 24 W R , 394

[2] *Welch v L & N.W Railway* [1885], 31 W R , 166

As an important decision, showing when luggage will be considered as being in the company's custody, so as to render them liable for its loss, I would call the reader's attention to the case of *Bunch v Great Western Railway Co.*,[1] where the facts were as follows. Mrs Bunch arrived at Paddington Station at 4.20 P M one Christmas Eve. She intended to go to Bath by the 5 P M. train, and had with her a portmanteau, a hamper and a Gladstone bag. A porter took the luggage, and Mrs Bunch saw it labelled, and said she wished the bag to be put into a compartment with her Upon the porter's assurance that it would be "all right," she went away to meet her husband, but on her return with him, after ten minutes' absence, the bag had disappeared.

The House of Lords, in giving judgment for plaintiff, said that the company could not shield themselves from liability by a public notice that their servants had orders not to take charge of any luggage or parcels, nor by a regulation in their time tables that they would not be liable for luggage taken with passengers into the carriages

When railway companies state they will not be liable for loss of or injury to luggage arising off their own lines, they will have to prove the luggage was lost or injured when *out of their custody*, and they will continue responsible if the loss or injury occurs at a station which they have the use of by agreement with another company.

[1] [1888] 13 *A C* , 31 , 57 *L J.Q B.*, 361.

It often happens that a servant is sent on in
advance with some of his employer's luggage, and
questions have arisen as to the extent of the
latter's right to sue the company for any loss
sustained by reason of such luggage being damaged
or delayed in transit.

In the case of *Meux v Great Eastern Railway
Co.*,[1] it appears that Lady Meux, who was moving
to her country residence, had sent on two servants
beforehand, with their liveries and a maid's dress
skirt valued at £23, which articles were not the
servants' property but belonged to Lady Meux
The things were destroyed owing to the negligence
of a porter in dropping them on to the line in
front of a train

The original judgment came in effect to this ·
Lady Meux could not recover compensation
because, although it was admitted that she had
supplied her servants with the money to buy their
tickets, yet the company had contracted only with
the servants, and were carrying the liveries as
their (the servants') luggage, and not as Lady
Meux's; and, further, that the servants could not
maintain an action because the liveries did not
belong to them, but were the property of Lady
Meux. In other words, the company were exempt
from liability for loss or damage to any luggage
which was not the personal property of the person
for whom the same was carried   The Court of

---

[1] [1895] 2 Q B , 369 , 64 L J Q.B , 657 , 73 L T , 247 , 43 W R ,
680 , 59 J P,, 662 , 14 R , 620

Appeal, however, took a more sensible view of the matter, holding that although Lady Meux could not sue in *contract* because she had never contracted with the company, and so there could not be any breach of contract, nevertheless she might sue *en tort*, on the ground that the act of the company's servants in dropping the liveries under the train was a misfeasance—a wrongful act, and one having nothing to do with any contract at all. Supposing, however, there had simply been an act of *omission*, *e.g.*, neglecting to put the luggage into the van, the judgment of the court of first instance would stand, and neither Lady Meux nor her servants could have successfully sued the company.

In an earlier case it had been decided that if a master takes a ticket for his servant to travel with him by train, the servant could maintain an action in his own name for the loss of his luggage.

Travellers have no right to take with them, free of charge, as if it were their own property, luggage which belongs to other people. The principles just referred to regarding a servant travelling with his master's luggage would not apply to this case, because the passenger would probably pay for his own ticket and not be servant of the owner of the luggage, but bailee of the luggage, either for reward or voluntary, according as to whether he did or did not receive anything for his trouble. In fact he would possess a limited kind of property in the luggage, whilst a mere servant would have no *property* whatever in goods entrusted to his care by his employer. The contract then being with the bailee, he would have the right to sue the company in respect of any damages sustained both by reason of the company's or their servants' nonfeasances or misfeasances (acts of omission or commission), and the owner of the luggage could sue for any misfeasances (acts of commission) only.

It should be remembered, however, that persons acting in this manner are in reality defrauding the company of the amount justly due for the carriage of the articles, and some railway companies have announced their intention of prosecuting such persons, but whether they could do so successfully would depend very much on the circumstances of the case.

Railway companies have the right to detain any luggage in their possession for an unpaid fare, but they have no right to sell any articles so detained

It has also been decided that if a man deposits a *hired* chattel in a railway cloak-room, and afterwards abandons it, the company have a lien thereon in respect of proper charges for the safe custody thereof, and may detain it till the same are paid, notwithstanding their knowledge that it was not the property of the depositor.

As regards articles deposited in a cloak-room, it may be mentioned that the company are under no obligation to warehouse luggage, and when thus warehoused the articles do not fall within the terms of that section of the Railway and Canal Traffic Act, 1854, referred to hereafter, requiring any special conditions on which luggage is carried to be just and reasonable and signed by the sender.

Railway companies refuse to warehouse anything except upon special conditions (printed on the ticket or receipt for the article deposited), such as, for example, that they decline to be responsible for any goods exceeding a certain value, usually £10; and it has been held that such a condition protects the company from liability for damage done to the article as well as against loss thereof. The depositor of goods will be bound by the conditions if he reads them without objection, or if he is aware there are conditions but does not trouble to read them, or purposely abstains from so doing, but not if he neither read the conditions nor knew of their existence.

It has been said by one judge that where a traveller puts a cloak-room ticket into his pocket without reading it he impliedly assents to its terms if they are reasonable, but otherwise not

In concluding this section of the chapter, I reproduce a portion of an article which appeared not long ago in the *Railway Magazine*, because, although not dealing with any point of law, the observance of the suggestions it contains may save not only travellers but also the railway companies a considerable amount of trouble and annoyance.

" Within recent years " (so the article proceeds) "some railway companies have introduced into their instructions a special injunction to the staff that in all cases of reported loss (of luggage) the owner's residence or place of departure is one of the earliest points at which inquiries must be instituted. Railway companies are frequently unnecessarily caused considerable trouble and expense in consequence of passengers omitting to remove old addresses or labels from their luggage before commencing a journey It is the opinion of all railway officials who have to deal with complaints of missing luggage that the obliteration or removal of labels would go far to minimise the inconvenience which travellers sometimes experience owing to the wrong sending of their property."

(b) Goods and Merchandise

With regard to goods or luggage other than "personal luggage," it may be observed that in olden times carriers were liable for the loss of or injury to articles of whatever value carried by them, provided such loss or injury was not attributable to the customer's own fault ($e.g.$, improper packing), the "act of God," the Queen's enemies, or the "inherent vice" of the thing carried

This liability at the present day affects railway companies (who are, of course, common carriers) in so far only as concerns goods *not* coming within the provisions of the Carriers Act, 1830.

The causes which led to the passing of this Act were —

(1.) The extreme hardship on carriers, who were frequently entrusted with things of great value, *e g*, jewellery, without being informed of the nature of the articles they were carrying, and who, in case of any loss happening thereto, became liable to pay heavy damages

(ii.) The uncertainties, so frequently arising, as to whether carriers had effectually got rid of their liability by posting up notices limiting such liability the question as to whether the carrier was or was not exempt from responsibility depending on whether or not the notice had come to the customer's knowledge.

By the Act in question it is enacted that carriers shall not be able to limit their liability at all by any public notice or declaration. The Act further provides that no carrier shall be liable for the loss of or injury to any articles such as gold or silver coins, jewellery, clocks, watches, etc ; bills, notes or securities for money, etc ; maps, stamps, writings, deeds, engravings, etc , glass, china, hand-made lace, etc , etc., delivered to be carried for hire, or *to accompany the passenger*, where the value thereof exceeds the sum of £10, unless at the time of delivering the same to be carried their value is declared and an increased sum paid, or agreed to be paid, in accordance with a scale of charges which must be exhibited in some conspicuous part of the carrier's office, and of which all persons delivering goods are to be deemed to have notice.

If required, a signed receipt must be given for the article acknowledging it to be insured

The " value" referred to means *actual value to the consignor*, so that if he is selling a painting to the consignee for £20, it would make no difference that the seller had been lucky enough to buy it the day before for £5 at a bankrupt sale; and where manufacturers allowed discount to a merchant who consigned jewellery to an intending purchaser, it was decided that such discount could not be deducted in order to bring the jewellery under the £10 limit.

Failure on the carrier's part to comply with the provisions as to exhibiting the scale of charges and giving a receipt will deprive him of the benefit of the Act, and, moreover, he will have to refund any increased charge paid

If the goods be lost or damaged, notwithstanding that their value has been declared and the increased charges paid, the party entitled to damages in respect thereof may recover also the amount of such increased charges.

The Act evidently has two objects in view, namely —

(i) To prevent, as to ordinary goods, carriers protecting themselves from liability by public notices, which, probably, their customers knew nothing of, but, at the same time, to allow carriers to make any terms they liked under a special contract

(ii.) On receipt of the article to at once apprise the carrier of its valuable nature, and thus enable him to bestow particular attention upon it, and also to give him additional compensation in consideration of the increased risk.

If the value has not been declared the carrier

is protected, although the loss be due to his gross negligence, and also in case of loss or damage incurred owing to the goods being negligently carried beyond their destination; and this whether the loss be permanent or merely temporary, and notwithstanding that the owner is obliged to replace them at an enhanced price.

There is a proviso that carriers are to remain liable for any felonious acts (e g , theft) of their servants, although the customer may *not* have declared and insured the goods. On the construction of this section it has been held[1] that it is only when the felonious act occurs by the company's negligence that the latter will be liable ; but that in case of theft by a servant, not in any way due to the carrier's negligence, the master escapes responsibility Nevertheless the servant remains answerable, and it is expressly provided by the Act that nothing therein contained is to protect any servant from liability for loss or injury caused by his own personal neglect or misconduct.

From the decisions on this subject it may be said that, generally speaking, the Act protects carriers against damages incurred by loss or destruction of or injury to the goods, whether the same be accidental or attributable to negligence, and also in those cases where it arises from the felonious act of a third party, or even of the carrier's servant, provided, in the latter case, the

[1] *Shaw v G.W Railway Co* [1894]. 1 Q B 373 , 70 L.T., 218 , 42 W R , 285 , 58 J P , 318 , 10 R , 65

felonious act occurs without the carrier's negligence

But it does not protect carriers if they or their servants wilfully or purposely do any act entirely inconsistent with the contract to carry, so that in such a case a railway company would be liable although the value of the goods had *not* been declared.

While the Act of 1830 thus abolished the efficacy of *public notices* limiting liability, it at the same time allowed carriers to make any special contracts with their customers regarding the conveyance of goods

Railway companies were by no means slow to take advantage of this provision, and after several decisions of the Courts holding that receipts given to persons delivering goods for carriage amounted to such special contracts as were contemplated by the section, and the legislature considering that in many instances these decisions bore very hardly on the customers, the Railway and Canal Traffic Act, 1854, was passed to remedy the grievances

This Act, though still permitting the making of special contracts, provides, by section 7, that nobody shall be bound by any such contract, unless—

(i) He or his agent has *signed* it

(ii) It is just and reasonable

As to whether a condition is "just and reasonable" under this section is for the judge at the trial to decide : and it would be useless to give here particulars of any of the numerous decisions, as many of them seem most contradictory In general, it may be said that conditions attempting to relieve railway companies from liability in respect of injury "however caused," or "in any case," and such conditions as are not framed with the intention of giving *bonâ fide* alternative rates of carriage, but with the view of giving *no* alternative, and thus practically compelling the consignor of the goods to adopt one rate in preference to another, are invalid.

The signature of the consignor of the goods will be binding under the Act, notwithstanding that he cannot read, and an agent's signature suffices

It appears (though the point is doubtful) that it is only necessary that the contract should be *signed* when the company want to protect themselves against neglect or default, and that if a purely accidental loss occurs a special contract protects the company, though neither signed nor reasonable

The Act also provides that railway companies shall not be liable for the loss of or injury to a horse beyond £50, neat cattle £15 a head, and pigs and sheep £2 per head, unless the same are, at the time of delivery to the company, declared to be of a higher value, and an increased rate paid in accordance with a tariff exhibited in manner prescribed by the Carriers Act, 1830 The onus rests on the party suing for damages to prove the animals were above the value specified in the Act

The consignee is, as a rule, the party to sue the

company for damages on account of negligence in the carriage of goods, as the contract is really with him, the consignor being considered as the consignee's agent to employ the railway company as carriers. But if the consignee has not acquired any property in the goods, then the consignor is the proper person to sue. The consignor may also sue when, by the contract between him and the railway company, the latter undertakes to deliver the goods to a particular person at a particular place, the contract thus doing away with the necessity of showing the ownership of the goods; also where the goods were sent only on approval, or where they were actually delivered to the company to be carried at the consignor's risk.

Railway companies must provide all reasonable facilities for despatching goods, but they are only bound to provide these facilities for such things as arrive in due time. In one case goods to be despatched by the 11 A.M. train reached the station at 11 1 A.M. The train was late, not in fact arriving till 11 8 A.M., but nevertheless the goods were not forwarded till a later train. Owing to the delay the sender lost his market at the place of their destination, but the company were held not liable.

The companies must convey the goods of all persons willing to pay the carriage (which must be of reasonable amount and uniform) without any unnecessary delay or deviation, and in the usual and customary course. They are not, however, bound to carry goods by the shortest route, but only by that by which they ordinarily carry such goods. But the company must not substitute one contract for another, and, after agreeing to convey the goods by one route, take them by another, and altogether different route. Thus, in a recent case, goods were carried at owner's risk by Great Eastern Railway to go forward to a certain place by Great Western Railway. Instead of being sent on by the Great Western they were forwarded per South Western, and in consequence the owner lost his market and suffered damage It was held that he could recover his loss from the company although, by the terms of the risk note, he had agreed not to sue, because the company had gone beyond the contract altogether, and had substituted another contract in its place, therefore the loss was not within the risk note

Damages can be recovered against a railway company for failing to deliver goods within a reasonable time If the consignee refuses the goods, in which case they would belong to the company, being thrown on their hands, the damages would be the value of the things at the place and time at which they ought to have been delivered If the goods are accepted, the damages would be the difference between the value thereof to the consignee at the time of delivery and the value the goods would have been had they been delivered in proper time.

The owner of goods cannot recover any special damages (*i.e.*, such damages as would not naturally be expected to be the result of the delay) unless he proves that when the goods were delivered to the company the circumstances out of which such loss arose were made apparent to them in a manner sufficient to lead one to suppose the goods were accepted subject to the condition that the company would be answerable for any special damages

In a well-known case,[1] decided in 1854, the facts were as follows Messrs. Hadley & Co. were Gloucester millers, the mill being worked by a steam engine In May, 1853, the crank shaft of the engine suddenly broke, thus stopping the mill Hadley & Co. at once wrote to a firm of engineers at Greenwich, and arranged to forward them the broken shaft, so that it might form a pattern for the new one. Plaintiffs then sent a servant to " Pickford & Co.," carriers, to fix for the broken shaft to be sent. A clerk at their office informed the servant that if the shaft was sent any day before noon it would be delivered in Greenwich the following day Next day the shaft was sent to defendants in good time, and the carriage paid in advance ; but it was not delivered at its destination the day after as had been represented Owing to this Hadley & Co. suffered heavy pecuniary loss, the mill remaining idle for some days, and so they brought an action to recover the profit which they would have made had the damaged shaft been delivered at Greenwich on the day stated. However, they did not succeed, it being held that if the carriers had been plainly told that

---

[1] *Hadley v. Baxendale*, 9 Ex , 341, 23 L. J. Ex , 179

a loss of profit would be the result of any delay on
their part they would have been liable, but that,
as it was not proved they were aware the want of
the shaft was the only thing keeping the mill idle,
they were not responsible, and that the damage
sustained by Messrs Hadley & Co was too remote
to be recoverable.

CHAPTER V.

THE CARRIAGE OF CYCLES.

CONSIDERING the large number of cycles now conveyed by train, no doubt a short chapter dealing with the subject of their carriage will interest many of my readers.

Every cycle carried by rail must have attached thereto a label stating its owner's name and destination—otherwise the company may refuse to accept it

In 1898 the Cyclists' Touring Club brought a test case[1] before the court, in the somewhat vain endeavour to obtain a decision that railway companies must carry cycles free of charge, as forming part of a traveller's " ordinary " luggage

It was held, however, that such articles, being of a special character and requiring particular care, are not only *not* " ordinary " or " personal " luggage, but are excluded from the designation of luggage altogether—the judges saying that by luggage was meant a thing which could be packed up in a box or bag, or something of that sort

However this may be, I think most people will agree that it would be unfair to expect railway

[1] *Britten v G N. Railway Co.* [1899], 1 Q B , 243, 68 *L J Q.B* , 75 , 79 *L.T.*, 640, 15 *T* , 71

companies to carry bicycles for passengers without some extra charge.

In an earlier case it had been decided that a commercial traveller in cycles, travelling with the component parts and with incomplete machines, is entitled to any special terms allowed by railway companies in respect of commercial traveller's luggage. But this decision had little or nothing to do with the point as to whether a bicycle was luggage, for the reason that the traveller did not carry complete machines, but only their component parts; and the question was not whether such parts were entitled to be carried as a passenger's ordinary luggage, but whether the company's special scale of charges for the luggage of commercial travellers applied thereto.

Cyclists must therefore pay for the carriage of their machines in accordance with the companies' fixed terms—a ticket being taken for the cycle and produced to any authorised servant of the company on demand.

Persons taking cycles by train without previously paying the fare for the carriage thereof, and with intent to avoid such payment, are liable to conviction for fraud.

But probably by far the most important point of law relative to the carriage of cycles is the extent of the company's liability in respect of any damage done to the machine whilst in course of transit.

Railway companies print on the back of their cycle tickets a notice to the effect that such articles are carried entirely at owner's risk, the companies disclaiming responsibility for any loss or damage whatsoever. From the careful consideration of various decisions, it seems clear that this condition is effectual to relieve the companies from liability, in so far as concerns any loss of or injury to the machine which is *not* attributable to the negligence of the companies or their servants, but that as regards any loss or damage resulting from negligence they cannot rid themselves of responsibility in this easy fashion, but the condition in order to be effectual must be duly *signed* by the owner of the cycle in accordance with the provisions of the Railway and Canal Traffic Act, 1854, mentioned in the last chapter. Moreover, even a signed condition, purporting to exempt the company from liability under all circumstances, or in the event of negligence, would probably be held to be unreasonable and not binding

CHAPTER V

ACCIDENTS

The subject of railway accidents is, of course, a very important one, and one on which a great deal might be said

I do not, however, think it would serve any useful purpose to enter at all fully into the matter in this lit l book, as to do so would occupy too much space, and it is fully dealt with in other works; moreover, I suppose anyone seriously injured in such an accident would place his case in the hands of a solicitor in order that it might be properly managed

I shall therefore confine my attention to a few important points, and to such as are likely to more often arise, referring those of my readers who desire to pursue the matter further to some larger book.

Railway companies, in the case of the carriage of passengers, are *not* in the position of insurers; and before a traveller can recover damages in respect of an accident happening to himself he must prove that it was the result of some negligence or breach of duty on the part of the company or their servants. Further, the passenger must not have been guilty of such contributory negligence as was really the direct cause of the accident occurring.

(85)

It is the duty of railway companies, as was laid down by the judges in the leading case of *Redhead v. Midland Railway Co.*,[1] to which I am about shortly to refer, "to take due care" (including in that term the use of skill and foresight) "to carry the passenger safely, and is not a warranty that the carriage in which he travels shall in all respects be fit for the purpose."

In general, however, it may be stated that the mere fact of an accident happening to a train, whilst under the exclusive control of the company's servants, raises the presumption that it was attributable to negligence, and on the company will lie the onus of refuting such presumption if they can, as, *e.g.*, by showing that the mishap was due to some latent defect in the construction of the carriages.

From the case just quoted it appears that the carriage in which Mr Redhead was travelling got derailed and upset owing to the breakage of one of the wheel tyres. The accident was due to a latent defect in the tyre, not attributable to any default on the manufacturer's part, and it could not have been detected prior to the breaking.

It was held, on appeal, affirming the decision of the court below, that the company were not liable, the cause of the accident being something altogether beyond their control.

It frequently happens, in the case of long trains, that some of the coaches do not at first get properly up to the platform, or else they run beyond it This is usually so with return excursion trains at intermediate stations, and a great many actions have been brought against railway companies by persons who have been injured in the attempt to get out under such circumstances

The mere fact of a train not coming properly up to the platform is no proof of negligence, but in such a case it at once becomes the duty of the company's servants to take what steps are necessary to prevent passengers alighting.

From the numerous decisions of the judges, it seems that the mere calling out of the name of the station is not necessarily an invitation to passengers to get out, but the bringing of the train to a standstill, after such time has elapsed as may reasonably lead the passengers to assume that they are expected to alight, is an invitation.

If a passenger, on the train stopping, thinks it has reached the station, and that he ought to get out, and proceeds to do so, and, owing to there being no platform, he hurts himself, the company will be responsible if the passenger had reasonable grounds for thinking and acting as he did

It has also been decided that although a traveller sees that his compartment has overshot or failed to reach the platform he is justified in descending, using proper care, provided no official comes to his assistance, and it appears that the train will depart without backing or drawing on as the case may be, and if he is injured the company will be liable

Of course, if the passenger does not choose to

get out, and so is carried on in the train, he will be entitled to recover his expenses, etc., from the company, as to which see *ante*, chapter iii

It is the duty of the company's servants to see that all carriage doors are securely fastened before the train leaves each station, and it has been held that a passenger is entitled to assume that the door is properly shut and to act accordingly. But if a door flies open anyone attempting to fasten it must act with due caution, and, if in trying to shut the door in order to avoid the inconvenience of having it open during the journey, the passenger runs into danger, the company would in many instances escape liability on the plea of contributory negligence

The author remembers reading of a case where a passenger who had fallen from a train owing to the door failing to " catch " properly was summoned by the company for " leaving the train whilst in motion and at a place not provided for passengers to alight "! The unfortunate traveller was actually convicted of the alleged offence and fined by some so-called "justices," but the conviction was afterwards quashed and damages recovered from the company.

Sometimes a passenger gets his hand or fingers crushed by the shutting of a carriage door by one of the company's servants, and questions have arisen as to how far the company can be made responsible in damages for such an occurrence

Often, no doubt, people have only themselves to blame for these accidents, which are generally due to their own carelessness in putting their fingers in places where they ought not to be, and the company's servants cannot be expected to look carefully to see that nobody's fingers are in the way before fastening each door. Of course if a porter sees that anyone has his fingers in the way, or recklessly slams doors before the passengers have had time to take their seats, the company would be liable, but not otherwise.

On this subject there have been three important decisions, to which I will now briefly refer.

In the first case, the guard of one of defendants' trains forcibly shut a carriage door without any warning, and in so doing crushed the hand of the plaintiff, who was *entering the carriage* The company were held liable because of their servant's negligence.

But where plaintiff left his hand on the edge of the door half a minute after entering the train, and on the shutting of the door his hand was injured, it was decided that he could recover no compensation, the accident being due to his own contributory negligence in leaving his hand on a door which he knew would be immediately shut, and but for his carelessness the accident could not have occurred.

In the third case, plaintiff was one of the occupants of a full compartment. Other passengers opened the door and attempted to force their way in. Plaintiff stood up to resist them. Whilst so standing with the door open, the train started, and he put his hand on the door lintel for support, at which moment a porter came up, turned away the intruders, and quickly shut the door in the usual manner, thereby crushing plaintiff's thumb

The House of Lords held that assuming the overcrowding to be due to the company's negligence, yet the injury was not nearly or certainly enough connected therewith to give plaintiff any cause of action, because (so said the Lords) the accident was one which might none the less have happened had there been no overcrowding at all.

Railway companies are liable for negligence causing injury to a passenger although he is travelling without a ticket, or has a ticket issued by another company, unless there was an intention on the passenger's part to defraud.

A newspaper reporter travelling with a free pass, and a child *above* three years of age carried free, have been held entitled to recover.

In one case, defendants, the Metropolitan District Railway Co., had running powers over the South-Western Railway Co , between Hammersmith and New Richmond, on the latter company's line Plaintiff took from the South-Western Co. a return ticket from Richmond to Hammersmith. The ticket was not headed with either company's name, but bore upon it the words "*via* District Railway".

On his return journey from Hammersmith plaintiff travelled with the ticket in a train belonging to defendants and under the control of their servants. The coaches being unsuitable for the platform at New Richmond Station, plaintiff, on alighting, fell and was injured

Subsequently he brought an action against the defendants, and the jury found the company guilty of negligence On appeal it was held that the company, having invited or permitted plaintiff to travel in their train, were bound to make reasonable provision for his safety, and that even *assuming the ticket was not issued by or for them* but for the South-Western Co., the defendants were nevertheless responsible for the occurrence.

Persons injured in railway accidents should be on their guard against being induced to accept a small sum of money from the company as compensation without first ascertaining the true extent of their injuries

It sometimes happens that the full effects of an accident do not make themselves immediately apparent, and if a passenger accepts a small sum (say £10), expressed to be " in full and complete satisfaction and discharge of all claims on account of, etc.," he will, in the absence of actual fraud on the company's part, experience great difficulty in afterwards suing them for damages should his injuries prove more serious than at first supposed. Nor, in such a case, would the passenger's representatives, in general, have any right to sue under the Fatal Accidents Act, 1846, in the event of his subsequently dying from the effects of the injury sustained.

However, a mere receipt in " discharge of claim in full " is not so conclusive as to preclude a passenger from suing the company for further compensation, and in all cases the question for the jury to decide is, " Did the passenger's mind go with the terms of the paper he signed ? "

Before 1846 it paid railway companies far better, pecuniarily, to kill a passenger outright in a collision than to merely maim him, because although in the latter case the injured traveller might have maintained an action against the company for damages, his representatives had no right to do so in the event of his being killed

This injustice was removed by the Fatal Accidents Act, 1846, providing that whenever the death of a person is caused by the wrongful act, neglect or default of another which would if death had not ensued have entitled the party injured to maintain an action in respect thereof, then the wrongdoer shall be liable to an action, although the circumstances amount in law to felony

It often happens that a person killed in a railway accident is in some way insured, and doubts have arisen as to whether the jury, in assessing damages under the Act referred to, are to take into consideration any moneys the representatives may receive from insurance companies.

Now, the object of the Fatal Accidents Act was to compensate the family of the deceased, that is, to put them in as far as possible the same *pecuniary position* in which they would have been had the passenger not been killed, and, in estimating the damages, grief, mourning and funeral expenses are not to be taken into account.

A travellei may have effected eithei —

(ı) An "accidental death" policy, or

(ıı.) An oıdınaıy life policy,

and it has been decided that ın each case a deduction must be made fıom the amount of damages the company would be lıable to pay, but such deduction will not be the same ın the two cases

Supposing an ordinary life policy has been effected. Heıe the repıesentatıves of the deceased will some day get the policy moneys, but on account of the ınsuıed's death by accident such moneys are forthcoming soonei than would have been the case had no accident occurred This being so, the juıy, ın calculating the damages, will have to deduct therefrom *not* the amount of the policy moneys, but only the estımated difference between gettıng the money at once instead of havıng to waıt for ıt In other words, the jury must deduct from the amount of compensation they consıder the company would have been lıable to pay ıf the passenger had dıed *unınsured*, the sum total, whıch, accordıng to the expectatıon of human lıfe, ıt might be assumed deceased would have paıd ın premiums had he not been kılled ın the accıdent.

The difference between the two sums is what the company will be lıable to pay

Supposıng, however, deceased has effected an "accıdental death" policy only, the case is different, because ıt will only be in the event of a death by *accıdent* that the policy moneys can ever become payable, and if there is no accident the representatives will never get a farthing.

Now, as has been pointed out, the object of the Fatal Accidents Act was to place the family of the deceased in as nearly as possible the same *pecuniary position* as if the latter were still alive, and the Courts have held that as if deceased's family receive the policy moneys and full damages besides they would be more than merely compensated—that, as in fact, they would be in a better position than before—the jury, in awarding damages, must deduct the whole amount received under the accidental death policy from the sum the railway company would have been liable to pay had there been no such policy in existence.

On the other hand, supposing a traveller who has effected an accidental *injury* policy to be hurt in a railway accident, it has been decided that *no* deduction whatever is to be made from the damages in respect of any insurance moneys received.

The reason for the distinction is, shortly, this · the *injured* passenger had always, as has been said (long before the Act of 1846 was passed), a right of action for damages, and the mere fact of his having made provision for the contingency of an accident occurring could in no way affect this right. In other words, although the passenger must get hurt in order to entitle him to the insurance money, yet he receives it not because of the accident, but because of his contract.

When, however, the legislature in 1846 gave a dead man's representatives a *statutory* right (a right they did not possess before) to recover damages in case deceased met his death in an accident, it was made clear that the intention was only to just compensate the family in a pecuniary sense, and in no way to doubly compensate them, nor, indeed, to compensate them at all in case they would occupy the same monetary position as before.

All this is admittedly very difficult to comprehend, and I should not have referred to it at all were it not that it is a matter of great importance, and one on which I have on two or three occasions been asked questions.

To further complicate matters, the Railway Passengers' Assurance Company got the following clause inserted in their Consolidation Act of 1892 "No contract of the company (*i.e.*, the Railway Passengers' Assurance Company), nor any compensation received or recoverable by virtue of any such contract under this Act or otherwise, shall prejudice or affect any right or action, claim or demand which any person or his legal personal representatives may have against any other company or any person, either at Common Law or by virtue of any Act of Parliament, for the injury, whether fatal or otherwise, in respect of which the compensation is received or recoverable ".

To sum up ·—

(1.) Insurance money is not to be wholly deducted in the case of an ordinary life policy, but only the estimated difference between getting the money immediately instead of at a future time.

(ii.) In the case of an "accidental death" policy, the money received thereunder is to be wholly deducted, unless indeed the policy is effected with the Railway Passengers' Assurance Company, or some other company (if any) possessing similar rights.

(iii) No deduction whatever is to be made in the case of an "accidental injury" policy.

Travellers and others may well ponder over this subject, and carefully consider whether in the event of their being unfortunately killed in a railway accident it will not be to the advantage of their dependants to insure with the Railway Passengers' Assurance Company in preference to any companies possessing no provision similar to the one referred to as regards damages. For surely, if the total amount of any insurance money is to be deducted from the damages to which a railway company may be liable, the insured will in reality have paid his premiums only to relieve the company from liability, and indeed in some instances the latter may escape scot free.

The same principles would apply to those insurances effected by purchasing a copy of *Pearson's Weekly* or *Answers*, for example.

Although therefore at the present day the gruesome tales of the guard going around immediately after a railway collision and gently tapping with a hammer the heads of those travellers who were badly injured have entirely ceased to be believed or told, the fact nevertheless remains that to a certain extent it *still pays railway companies* to kill their passengers instead of seriously injuring them, as, if insured against accidental death, the companies often escape liability to the extent of the sums received under the policy, whereas, if merely insured against injuries, the companies can get no advantage from any amount the insured receives in respect thereof

CHAPTER VII

SOME MISCELLANEOUS POINTS

A RAILWAY carriage forming part of a train is a public place, and passengers playing any game of chance therein for money run the risk of three months' imprisonment under the Vagrant Act[1]

If, however, an entire compartment is reserved for the players, no offence would be committed, the compartment then becoming a *private* place, as the occupants would have the right to eject any intruders (using no unnecessary force) on their refusal to quit

All large or heavy luggage ought to go in the van "The racks are provided for light articles only, and must not be used for heavy luggage." In practice, however, very heavy articles are often placed upon the racks, which usually seem strong enough to bear them, and it is doubtful if the company could successfully sue a passenger for damaging the rack unless, indeed, it could be proved the luggage was wilfully placed thereon after the traveller had been warned against so doing, or that he had good reason to believe that it would damage the rack.

[1] 5 Geo. IV., cap 83, *Langrish* v *Archer* [1882], 52 *L.J.M.C.*, 47, 102 *B.D* 44, 47 *L T* (*N S*) 548, 31 *W R* 183

Passengers should be careful how they place their luggage on the racks, as if placed negligently, and a fellow-traveller is injured by some article falling upon his head, for example, the owner would have to make him compensation

It would be otherwise if there was no negligence in depositing the luggage, or if it appeared perfectly safe, and fell owing to a sudden jolt in the running of the train   The railway company, and not the traveller, would be liable in damages if the rack was negligently left in an insecure condition, of which the owner of the luggage was unaware. Probably also the company would be responsible for the negligent placing of luggage by a porter, unless it could be proved that in so placing it he was doing something entirely outside the scope of his employment.

Many people have a by no means unnatural dislike to put their belongings anywhere except on the seats, where they will have them constantly before their eyes, and thus minimise the risk of forgetting them when leaving the train ; but in so doing they must not act in such a manner as to inconvenience other passengers   One sometimes sees, especially in second class carriages, a passenger seated in one corner of a compartment and a parcel deposited in each of the others, as if to indicate that the occupant considers the whole compartment as appropriated to his own selfish use.   In a case of this sort any other traveller desiring a corner seat has a perfect right to remove such obstacles, nor will it make any differ ence if they have to be placed on the rack or floor, that is, assuming there to be no vacant seats left, the latter being provided for the accommodation of passengers, and not for the baggage of those individuals occasionally met with who make no offer to remove their belongings on other passengers entering the compartment.

At the same time, in order to avoid as far as possible any unpleasantness, it is as well, where there is any doubt on the matter, to inquire whether the seat is already appropriated by some one else, as travellers have, by custom, a legal right to retain their seats during any temporary absence. In a County Court case, decided in 1897, a passenger journeying from London to Hastings alighted for a few moments at Tunbridge Wells, leaving in his place a magazine and an umbrella, and also a bag on the rack just overhead. Despite these indications of prior occupancy somebody else took possession of the seat, and absolutely declined to vacate on request, whereupon he was ejected, and subsequently brought an action against the first passenger to recover £10 10s. damages for assault and battery. The latter counterclaimed for the same amount. The judge held there was an obvious necessity for travellers to occasionally leave their seats, and that the only question remaining for him to decide was whether the former occupant had left sufficient indications of prior possession. His Honour considered the magazine, umbrella and bag amply sufficient, and further found that their owner was entitled to use reasonable force in order to regain his seat, and, on those grounds, non-suited the plaintiff and sustained the counter-claim. This decision would also cover the case of an intending passenger arriving at the station a short time before the departure of his train and placing a bag or other article on a seat It must be remembered, however, that no greater amount of force should be used than is absolutely essential in order to turn out intruders, otherwise the ejector may himself become liable to pay heavy damages.

Passengers expecting friends to join the train at intermediate stations have no right to retain seats for them if there is no other room, nor, probably, whether there is other room in the train or not. The plan of locking the carriage door is some-times resorted to under these circumstances. or where passengers want a compartment to them-selves, but unless the same has been duly engaged any other traveller has the right to have it un-locked on lack of room elsewhere

Railway companies are in no way responsible for articles left, whether accidentally or by design, in the carriages or waiting rooms, or upon the platforms, in the event of their being lost or stolen. The companies usually assert that every-thing found on their premises and not claimed within a certain time becomes their own property. This, however, is not so, and the law on the sub-ject may be briefly summarised as follows —

All articles found by the company's servants whilst on duty and in the course of their employ-ment become, if not claimed by the rightful owners,

the property of the company, and the servant finding them has no right thereto as against the company

But if the servant is *off duty*, or the finder is a
passenger or other person lawfully on any part of
the company's premises being a public place (*e g.*,
in a carriage, or refreshment room, or on a platform), he will be entitled to anything he may be
lucky enough to find in case the true owner is not
forthcoming

Examples —

(1) X, a porter, whilst sweeping out a carriage,
finds a gold ring. If the ring is not claimed by its
owner it will become the property of the company,
as the finding of the porter was in fact the finding
of his employer—the railway company.

(ii.) X finds the ring whilst travelling home
after his day's work. He can claim the ring if
the owner is not forthcoming, as he did not find it
in the course of his employment

(iii.) B, a passenger, finds a purse on the seat
of a compartment in which he is travelling. B is
entitled to the purse if the true owner does not
claim it, the passenger having lawfully found it in
a place to which the public have a right of access.

(iv) B, passing a set of empty coaches at a
station platform, and seeing a purse on one of the
seats, enters the compartment and takes possession
of the purse. B cannot retain it as against the
company, because the place in which he found it
was *not, at the time of finding*, a public place, but a
private place, from which the company had the

right to exclude unauthorised persons. It need hardly be added that it is the duty of the finder of an article of any real value to take proper steps to ascertain its owner. The company should be immediately apprised of the finding of any valuables, in order that they may be restored to the owner, who will presumably make inquiry of the company with regard thereto. Further, anyone detaining a lost chattel may be sued for its return by the rightful owner, and the finder cannot *legally* demand any reward other than his out-of-pocket expenses, if any.

If the finder, *at the time of finding* the article, has reasonable grounds of belief as to who the owner is, or that he can be found, *and* intends to, and simultaneously with the finding appropriates it to his own use, he will be guilty of larceny. But these two essentials must be combined in order to constitute this crime, and the mere belief that the owner can be ascertained, without the intention *at the time of finding* to convert the article to his own use, will not make the finder legally a thief, nor will the intention to so appropriate it, if there be no reasonable belief that the owner can be ascertained.

Regarding loose coin found "under the cushions of the seats," as is sometimes said to be the case, this would generally constitute such a complete abandonment of the money by its owner as to entitle the finder to appropriate it for himself without making any inquiries.

Although, usually, no criminal proceedings can

be taken against persons for trespass unaccompanied by *wilful damage*, or unless the trespass can be said to be in "pursuit of game"—and the notice boards one so often sees announcing that "all persons found trespassing will be prosecuted" have not inappropriately been termed "wooden liars"—yet railway companies have statutory powers of taking Police Court proceedings against persons wilfully trespassing on the railway and refusing to quit immediately on the request of an official to do so. A conviction entails a fine not exceeding £5, or a month's imprisonment in default Also, any person who has once received warning from the company or their servants not to go or pass on the railway, doing so, except to cross at an authorised crossing, is liable to a penalty of £2, with the alternative of a month's imprisonment Persons loitering about stations or in waiting rooms, and not being ticket holders or intending passengers or having other business in the station, are, of course, trespassers, and liable to conviction

In the ordinary case of a person charged with trespassing and doing wilful damage, or trespassing in pursuit of game, if the defendant sets up as a defence a claim of right or title to go upon the land, and there is, apparently, some *bonâ fide* and reasonable ground for such claim, the jurisdiction of the magistrates is taken away, and they cannot deal with the case. But this, it has very recently been held, does not apply to railway companies' property, because of the express provision contained in the Regulations of Railways Act, 1840, and therefore the justices can inquire into, and decide upon, the question as to whether the alleged right really exists

Persons who make use of the means of communication between passengers and the servants of the company in charge of the train without reasonable and sufficient cause are liable to a penalty of not exceeding £5 for each offence   As to what would constitute "reasonable and sufficient cause " is for the passenger, and in some instances also for the magistrates, to determine from the facts of each case   There would certainly be reasonable and sufficient cause for a traveller thus stopping the train to prevent some injury being done to himself or others by a drunkard or lunatic, for example; or if the train failed to stop at a station marked as a regular stopping station and at which the traveller wished to alight ; but not if it was merely a " conditional " stopping place, and the passenger had omitted to tell the guard he wanted to get out there ; nor if the passenger had by his own negligence entered a train which he found was taking him in the wrong direction.

The Railway Clauses Consolidation Act, 1845, contains the important enactment that no person shall be entitled to carry, or require the company to carry, on the railway any aquafortis, oil of vitriol, gunpowder, lucifer matches, or any other goods which in the judgment of the company may be of a dangerous nature , and if any person send by the railway any such goods without distinctly marking their nature on the outside of

the packet containing the same, or otherwise
giving written notice to the servant of the company
with whom the same are left at the time of so
sending them, he shall forfeit to the company £20
for every such offence; and it shall be lawful for
the company to refuse to take any parcel they
may suspect to contain goods of a dangerous
nature, or require the same to be opened to ascertain the fact

The same Act provides that if any person pulls
down or injures any board put up or affixed for the
purpose of publishing any bye-law or penalty, or
shall obliterate any of the letters or figures thereon, he shall forfeit for every such offence a sum
not exceeding £5, and shall defray the expenses
attending the restoration of such board

It may also be mentioned that any person
opening a gate at a level crossing to pass through,
or otherwise, and failing to shut and fasten it
again, is liable to a penalty of £2.

Until recently there was some difference of
opinion as to the rights of passengers to obtain
intoxicating liquors at railway station refreshment
rooms during the hours when licensed premises
are required by law to be closed for the sale of
drink to other than *bonâ fide* travellers The
Licensing Act, 1874, contains the proviso that
" nothing in the Licensing Acts as to hours of
closing shall preclude the sale at any time at a
railway station of intoxicating liquor to persons
arriving at or departing from such station by railroad "

In the case of *Williams* v. *McDonald*,[1] Williams, on Sunday, 6th November, 1898, was in the refreshment room at Cymmer Station at 9·40 A.M., and representing that he intended to go by train to Blaen Gwynfy, another station on the railway two miles distant, obtained a glass of ale from the servant of the company in charge of the room. He had produced to an inspector of police a ticket to Blaen Gwynfy, and he did, in fact, travel by the next train, leaving at 9 48 A.M. The place where Williams had lodged during the previous night was within three miles of the refreshment room. The justices found that defendant was not a *bonâ fide* traveller at the time he obtained the ale, and that he got the ticket and entered the train for the express purpose of obtaining intoxicating liquor, and on these grounds convicted him. Williams, however, appealed, and the conviction was unanimously quashed, because the Act does not provide that the person obtaining the drink must travel *for business*, and that having taken a ticket, and actually going by the train, he was a traveller without doubt—in fact he came within the very letter of the Act—for nobody could deny that he was a person "departing from" the "station by railroad"; and it therefore was quite immaterial to consider whether he travelled for business or pleasure or simply in order to get a drink. It should be remembered, however, that anyone going

---

[1] [1899] 2 *Q B* , 308 , 68 *L J.Q B* , 678 , 80 *L T* , 758 , 47 *W.R* , 701 , 15 *T* , 343.

to ordinary licensed premises during closing hours solely to get liquor is liable to conviction, notwithstanding the place where he passed the night was *beyond* the three mile limit.

The fares to those places to which passengers are booked direct must be published by exhibiting a list of them at the booking offices of each station If the fare to any station be stated on the list, the company are bound to carry travellers tendering the amount thereof for the sum named Railway companies sometimes demand a higher fare, or say they cannot book the passenger through, or only by a route other than that specified. It is almost needless to say that by so acting the company are, on the clearest principles of law, committing a gross breach of contract. Travellers should, therefore, refuse to pay any higher fare, and demand tickets by the route named If more than the advertised fare is paid, the excess can be recovered.

Every ticket must now have the fare legibly printed or written thereon, or otherwise the company are liable to a penalty of £2 in respect of each ticket lacking such information.

Railway companies have to pay duty to Government on all first and second class tickets issued, and it was held not long ago that the selling of "third class reserved" tickets was a mere device to escape the duty, and that it would have to be paid

Questions sometimes arise between passengers as to their rights regarding the opening or closing

of the carriage windows. It is the generally understood thing that those travellers occupying the
corner seats immediately facing the respective windows have, *within all reasonable limits*, the right of
control over them.

It should be borne in mind that in a compartment containing six or eight persons there must
necessarily be some diversity of opinion concerning the window question, and that no passenger,
or majority of passengers, have the right to insist
on the windows being either wholly "up" or
"down" Indeed, considering that every compartment has two windows with window straps, each
of which (unless it has been "cut down" by some
evil disposed person, thereby rendering himself
liable to a penalty of £2) has from three to five
holes, provided for the adjustment of the sashes,
there should be no difficulty in suiting the require-
ments of all the occupants

The Court of Wyane (U S.A.) has held that
railway companies must carry fresh air "free,'
so to speak, and that in case it is impossible to
open a window the traveller is entitled to break
the glass in order to secure ventilation.

The same would probably be held in this
country.

As most people will be aware it sometimes
happens that in dry and hot weather considerable
damage is occasioned to property adjacent to railways, owing to sparks emitted from the locomotives
causing a conflagration. Railway companies are
not answerable for any damage thus incurred,

provided they have authority to use such engines, and, in so doing, have exercised proper care.

On this subject there have been two very interesting and instructive decisions, to which I will briefly refer

In the first case,[1] a Mr. Vaughan was owner of a plantation adjoining the Taff Vale Railway Company's embankment One hot dry day a spark from a locomotive set fire to and burned eight acres of the plantation which was of a very combustible nature It was decided that the company were not liable, because they were authorised to use the engines, and had adopted every precaution science could suggest to avoid injury

In the second case [2] the facts were as follows: Dry weather had continued for a considerable period, and a strong south-east wind was blowing at the time of the accident. About a fortnight earlier the company's servants had been cutting the grass and hedges on the embankments On the morning of the fire, the cuttings, which were very dry, had been collected into heaps and laid on the bank inside the hedge. Near to the hedge was a stubble field, beyond the field a road, and on the other side of the road was a cottage, two hundred yards distant from the railway. Shortly after a train had passed, the grass between the railroad and hedge was observed to be in flames, and, notwithstanding all efforts to extinguish it, burned

---

[1] [1860] 5 H. & N , 679 , 29 L J. Ex , 247
[2] [1870] 6 C.P , 14

through the hedge and field, and ultimately set fire to the cottage It was held that the company, on account of their negligence, considering the dry weather, in leaving the inflammable cuttings in such a dangerous position, were liable for the consequential damage, although their locomotives were of the best possible construction and fitted with the most approved appliances for preventing accidents.

In the absence of negligence, railway companies are not liable for damages suffered owing to a horse taking flight at the sight of one of their engines.

A person whose land has *not* been taken for the purposes of a railway can recover no compensation from the company in respect of damages arising from vibration occasioned, without negligence, by the running of trains, although the value of the property has been actually depreciated thereby

In the absence of some agreement, or established custom to the contrary, it is not the duty of anybody to erect fences for the purpose of keeping his neighbour's cattle *out*, the legal responsibility resting on all persons to fence their beasts *in*, and thus prevent them trespassing on other people's property ; but railway companies are specially required by statute to make and maintain fences, etc., for the accommodation of the occupiers of adjoining lands. In the event of any loss arising from breach of this duty the company will be liable in damages.

It has been held that the fences must be sufficiently strong to keep out swine, although these animals require a more substantial kind of fence than cattle. But supposing cattle first *stray into a field adjoining the line*, and then get on to the line and are killed, it has been decided that the company escape liability, for if the owner of the animals had properly fenced them out of his neighbour's land the accident could not have happened.

By statutory enactment any person employed on a railway who—

(i.) Is found drunk while so employed; or,

(ii.) Infringes the company's bye-laws, or,

(iii.) Wilfully or negligently does or omits to do any act whereby life or limb may be endangered, or traffic interrupted, is liable to a £10 fine or two months' imprisonment.

Considering the frequent attempts to wreck trains which have been made during the last two or three years, it may be well to mention that under the Malicious Injuries to Property Act, 1861, it is felony, the maximum penalty for which is penal servitude for life—

(i.) To put or throw upon or across any railway any wood, stone, or other thing

(ii.) To take up, remove or displace, any rail, sleeper, or other thing belonging to a railway

(iii.) To move or divert any points or other machinery belonging to any railway.

(iv.) To make or show, hide or remove, any signal or light upon or near any railway.

(v.) To do or cause any other thing to be done with intent to endanger the safety of passengers

(vi) To throw against or into any railway engine, carriage or truck any wood, stone, or other thing, with intent to injure or endanger the safety of any person in the train

By the same Act it is a misdemeanour, punishable by two years' imprisonment, for any person, by any unlawful act or wilful omission or neglect, to obstruct any engine or carriage in use on the railway   The alteration of a signal, or holding up the arms in the manner used by railway servants, is sufficient obstruction to bring the case within the Act

Many travellers may be unaware that railway companies have in their employ a large number of detectives and police in order to protect themselves from the innumerable cases of fraud, theft, etc , continually being attempted and often successfully carried out in the trains and upon the companies premises   The following is extracted from the *Railway Magazine* for February, 1900.   "The erroneous notion that railway detectives are merely ornamental accessories of the service, with no power to act summarily in the event of detection, is confined to innocent and unoffending citizens   The 'sharpers' and 'dodgers' of modern society know better than this, and do not run too close a risk in the immediate vicinity of the guardians of the law. As a matter of fact many members of the staff are 'sworn' men, and possess similar powers and privileges to the metropolitan, city

and municipal police   Some railways have powers
under their Acts of Parliament to swear in a
proportion of their police, while others, by the
courtesy of the borough magistrates throughout
their districts, are enabled to equip themselves
with officers endowed with corresponding jurisdiction to the local constabulary "

INDEX

Abusive Language, 37

Accident,

passenger not liable for damage done by unavoidable, 35

company liable for, if negligent, 85

presumption of negligence if train under company's control, 86.

through carriage not coming to platform, 86, 87

hand or finger crushed by carriage door, how far company liable for, 88 90

company liable for, though passenger without ticket, 90, 91

person injured should be slow to accept compensation, 91

receipt in discharge of claim re, 91, 92

pays company better to kill in, than injure, 97

Accidental Damage,

passenger doing, not liable, 35

Accidental Policy,

how far, benefits company, 92-97.

Additional Fare,

passenger travelling beyond station to which booked must pay, 4, 24-26.

but not liable to pay " difference in fares, ' 24, 25

re excursion tickets, 26-30.

Address

See " Name "

Air,

fresh, in carriages, 108, 109

Alteration, Train,

notice of, required, 54-56

Animals.

See " Cattle," " Dogs," " Horses," " Sheep, ' " Pigs "

Annoyance,

at late train, no damages for, 50

APPOINTMENT,
    loss of, through late train, generally no remedy for, 53, 54.

ARREST,
    company's police empowered to, 113, 114
    and see " Detention "

ASSAULT,
    interesting cases on, 2, 16, 100

BAD LANGUAGE,
    using, on company's premises, 37

BANK HOLIDAYS,
    trains suspended on, 58, 59

BICYCLE,
    carried by rail requires label, 82
    not luggage, 82, 83
    traveller with component parts entitled to special terms for
        commercial travellers' luggage, 83
    taking by rail, fare unpaid, 83
    when company liable for damaging, 83, 84

BOARD,
    notice, damaging, 106

BOOKING PASSENGER
    company contract to carry with reasonable despatch, 49.
    company must book through if connection shown, and at fare
        and by route specified, 50, 108

BOOKINGS,
    through, list of, must be exhibited, 108

BREAKING JOURNEY
    See " Journey "

BROKEN WINDOW, 34-36

BUSINESS ENGAGEMENT,
    loss of, through late train, generally no compensation, 53, 54.

BYE-LAWS CITED,
    being intoxicated or using bad language, etc., 37
    damaging property, 34
    defacing ticket, 20
    dogs, conveyance of in carriages, 37
    entering, etc , carriage in motion, 21

BYE LAWS CITED—*continued*
    entering full compartment, 16
    infectious disorder, travelling with, 36
    loaded firearms, bringing on railway premises, 37
    smoking, 22
    ticket, defacing, 20.
        „   obtaining and delivering up, 6
        „   issued conditionally at intermediate stations, 11, 12
        „   using for other station, 24
        „   „   superior class, 31
        „   return, sale or purchase of, 11
    travelling on roof, steps, etc , 20
BYE-LAWS,
    essentials for validity of, 5, 6
    require sanction of Board of Trade, 6
    must be published at stations, 6
    names of persons infringing may be published, 38 40
    company's servants infringing, 112

CAB FARE,
    when company liable for, 49, 51, 61
CARDS,
    offence to play, for money in train unless compartment engaged, 98
CARRIAGE,
    damaging, 34-36, 109
    not coming to platform, passenger injured in alighting, 87
    door of, unfastened, 88
    hand crushed by door of, 88 90
    offence to play cards for money in, 98
    when a public place, 98
CARRIERS,
    Act, 1830, 72-76
    railway company common, of goods, 72
CATTLE,
    company's liability for, 77
    trespassing, 111, 112
CHANGES IN TRAINS
    See " Alteration '

CHEAP TICKETS,
  company need not issue, 29
  conditions on, when valid, 26 31
  due notice of withdrawal of, required, 57, 58.
CLASS,
  no room in superior, 12, 14
  riding in superior, 31-34
CLOAK-ROOM,
  hired chattel left in, lien on, 70
  ticket, condition limiting liability, 71
COACHES
  See "Carriage" and "Platform"
COMMUNICATION CORD,
  using, 105
CONDITION,
  passenger must know of, or have means of knowing of, to be
      bound, 27.
  on excursion ticket, 27
  on cloak-room ticket, 71
  in case of carriage of goods, requisites for, 76
CONTRACT TICKET.
  See "Season Ticket".
  special for carriage of goods, essentials for, 76
  company cannot substitute, 79
CONVICTED PERSONS,
  publishing list of, 38 40
COSTS
  See "Expenses"
CURTAIN,
  damaging, 34
CUSHION,
  damaging, 34
  not for luggage, 99, 100
CYCLE
  See "Bicycle"

DAMAGES,
  for lateness of train, 47, 48, 54
  for not delivering goods in time, 79 81
  special, when recoverable, 79 81

DAMAGING COMPANY'S PROPERTY, 34-36

DANGEROUS GOODS,
    sending by rail, 105, 106

DECLARATION,
    limiting liability for carriage of goods invalid, 73, 76.

DEFACING,
    ticket, 20
    number plate, 34.

DEFAULT,
    wilful, what is, 47.
    See also Addenda

DEPOSIT ON SEASON TICKET,
    when, forfeited, 43

DEFECTIVE,
    railway, 113, 114

DETENTION,
    of passenger without ticket, 2, 4, 5
    by lateness of train, 46 51
    See also Addenda

DIFFERENCE IN FARE,
    passenger not liable to pay, 24, 25

DISAPPOINTMENT,
    through late train, no damages for, 50

DISCONTINUANCE,
    of train, company liable for not giving notice of, 56 59

DISEASE,
    infectious, travelling with, 36.

DOGS,
    not allowed in carriages, 37.

DOOR,
    carriage, unfastened, 88.
    passenger's hand crushed by, 88-90

DRINK,
    obtaining, at station during closing hours, 106-108

DRUNK,
    on company's premises, 37.
    in company's service, 112

ENGAGEMENT,
    business, loss of, through late train, 53, 54

ENTERING,
    full carriage, 16-18
    train in motion, 21
EXCURSION TICKETS,
    special conditions re, 26
    not available at intermediate stations, 27
    probably may be "excessed," 27 30.
    company need not issue, 29
    not available on other than days named, 31
EXPENSES,
    cab and hotel, recoverable, 49, 51, 61, 88
    incurred through train delay, 49, 61, 88
    to render company liable for, must be natural consequence of
        delay, 49, 61, 88
    must be reasonably incurred, 51, 61, 88
EXPRESS,
    stopped at small station by signal, passenger mistaking, for
        local train, 60

FARE,
    bye law requiring passenger without ticket to pay from where
        train started is void, 6, 7
    "additional" not "difference" payable for additional distance,
        4, 24 26.
    excess, in case of excursion ticket, 26-30
    stated, company must carry for, 50, 108
FARES,
    to be published at stations, 108
    to be stated on tickets, 108
    supplemental, cannot be charged unless duty paid, 108
FINDER,
    of lost property, duty of, 103
FINGER,
    crushed by shutting door, 88-90
FIRE,
    caused by engine spark, 109 111.
FIRE-ARMS,
    loaded, bringing, on company's premises, 37.
FOG,
    company not liable if delay due to, 48

FRAUD,

> giving up out-of-date ticket not evidence of, 10
>
> riding superior class, when evidence of, 31-34
>
> how to act to avoid semblance of, 34

FRESH AIR

> See "Ventilation"

FRONT PART TO LIVERPOOL, ETC,

> passenger in wrong part, 61

FULL COMPARTMENT,

> entering, 16

GATE,

> penalty for not shutting, 106

GOODS,

> company common carriers of, 72
>
> company's liability for, 72-77
>
> liability for cannot be limited by notice, 73
>
> valuable, when company not liable for, 73.
>
> theft of, 75
>
> condition on receipt for, will not limit liability, 76
>
> special contracts for carriage of, 76, 77
>
> loss of, etc, who to sue, 78.
>
> reasonable facilities for despatch of, required 78, 79
>
> of all persons must be carried, 78, 79
>
> route of carriage of, must not be changed, 79
>
> must be delivered in due time, 79.
>
> delay in delivery of, what damages for, 79-81
>
> dangerous, 105, 106

GUN,

> loaded, on company's premises, 37

HAND,

> crushed by shutting door, 88-90

HOLIDAYS,

> bank, trains suspended on, 58, 59

HORSE,

> company's liability for, 77
>
> frightened at train, 111.

HOTEL,

> expenses, when recoverable, 49, 51, 61, 88

INCONVENIENCE,
    by overcrowding actionable, 14, 15.
    company liable for, 50, 51

INFECTIOUS DISEASE,
    travelling with, 36.

INFERIOR CLASS,
    passenger obliged to travel in, return of fare, 11, 12.
    when actionable to put passenger of, into superior, 16.

INSURANCE
    of valuables, when necessary, 73, 74
    policies may relieve company from liability for fatal accident
        92-95
    with Railway Passengers' Assurance Company, 95, 96

INTERMEDIATE STATION,
    what is, 13.
    tickets issued at, conditionally, 11, 12.
    journey not to be broken at, 25
    excursion ticket forfeited if used at, 27

INTOXICATING LIQUOR
    See " Drink".

JOURNEY,
    passenger may not break, 25
    unreasonable delay on, 49

" JUST AND REASONABLE " CONDITION,
    what is, 76

KILL,
    pays better to, in accident, 92 97.

LAND,
    compulsorily taken, 5, 111

LATE TRAINS, 46-48

" LAW NOTES,"
    moot points, 16, 18

LEAVING TRAIN IN MOTION, 21

LIABILITY,
    for carriage of goods, 73-76
    for damaging cycle, 83, 84

LIBEL,
    not a, to publish names of convicted persons, 39, 40

LIGHT ARTICLES,
    racks for, 98, 99
LIQUOR.
    See " Drink ".
LOADED FIRE-ARMS
    See " Gun ".
LOST,
    ticket, 7
    property, 101-104.
LUGGAGE,
    carried free, 62
    excess, paid for, 62.
    " personal," what is, 63
    when company liable for, 64
    must be ready for delivery at journey's end, 64
    when company not liable for, 64-67
    handed to porter, depends on circumstances whether company
        liable, 65-67
    lost off company's line, 67
    servant carrying master's, 68, 69
    servants', 69
    carrying other people's, 69, 70
    detention of, for unpaid fare, 70
    in cloak-room, lien on, 70.
    how to avoid losing, 71, 72
    bicycle is not, 82, 83
    on racks, 98, 99
    passenger hurt by fall of, 99
    seats not for, 99 100

MATCHES
    See " Dangerous Goods".
MEAL,
    when company must pay for, 61, 88
MERCHANDISE.
    See " Goods' and " Luggage "
MOOT POINTS, 16, 18, 58
MOTION,
    entering or leaving train in, 21

NAME, ETC,
>   passenger refusing, etc., 1 5.
>   of convicted person may be published, 38-40

NEGLECT,
>   wilful, what is, 47
>   *See* also Addenda

NEGLIGENCE,
>   in carriage of goods, who to sue, 77, 78
>   presumption of, on accident, 86
>   *See* "Accident"

NOTICE,
>   of change in train service, 54 58
>   public, company cannot limit liability by giving, 73 76
>   board, damaging, 106

NUMBER PLATE,
>   removing, 34

OBSTRUCTING OFFICER OF COMPANY, 40
OFFICER OF COMPANY,
>   who is, 3

ORDINARY,
>   ticket, *see* "Ticket"
>   luggage, as to, 62 *et seq*

OVERCROWDING,
>   company liable to action for, 14, 15
>   passenger robbed in train through, company not liable for refusing to detain train, 15

PASSENGER,
>   without ticket, what to do, 8
>   lost ticket, what to do, 8
>   too late to book, what to do, 8.
>   given up ticket in error, what to do, 9
>   given up wrong half ticket, what to do, 9
>   can be prevented riding without ticket, 8
>   using out-of date ticket 9
>   no room for, fare returned, 11.
>   obliged to ride in inferior class, 11
>   entering full carriage, 16

PASSENGER—*continued*,
    entering or leaving train in motion, 21
    entitled to keep seat and eject intruders, 100, 101
    accident to, *see* " Accident "

PASSENGERS,
    Railway, Assurance Company, 95, 96

PERSONAL,
    inconvenience, company liable for, 50, 51.
    luggage, as to, 62 *et seq*

PIGS,
    extent of company's liability for 77
    company must fence against trespass by, 111

PILLORY,
    the railway, what it is, 38-40

PLATFORM,
    covered, penalty for smoking on, 22
    train starting from different, company must inform passengers
        59.
    coaches not coming to, 87

POLICE,
    railway, 113.

PORTER,
    not an " officer " with power to detain, 3
    risk of handing luggage to, 65-67

PORTIONS,
    train divided into, passenger in wrong, 61.

PUBLIC PLACE,
    railway carriage is, 98

PUBLICATION,
    of offenders' names, no remedy against company, 38-40

RACKS,
    for light articles only, 98, 99

RAILWAY,
    company, common carrier of goods, 72
    and Canal Traffic Act. 1854, 76
    trespass on, 104
    and *see* " Passenger," " Ticket," " Train ".

RAILWAYS,
    Regulation of, Act, 1889, 1-5, 25.

RECEIPT,
    for goods, conditions on, 71, 76
    in discharge of claim for accident, 91
REFRESHMENT-ROOM,
    penalty for smoking in, 22
    company liable for allowing smoking in, 23.
    obtaining drink at, during closing hours, 106-108.
REGULATION OF RAILWAYS ACT, 1889, 1-5, 25
RETURN TICKET,
    out-of-date, not available, 9, 10
    using out-of-date, not evidence of fraud, 10
    penalty for transferring, 11
RIDING,
    on roof or steps, 20
    in superior class, 31-33.
ROBBERY,
    in train through overcrowding, company not liable for refusing
        to detain train, 15
ROOF,
    riding on, 20
ROOM,
    lack of, fare returned, 11
    not guaranteed at intermediate stations, 11

SCRATCHING WINDOW
    penalty for, 34
SEASON TICKET,
    a contract, 41
    company need not issue, 42
    penalty for transferring, 42
    holder must carry, or pay fare, 42, 43
    deposit on, when forfeited, 43
    holder sued for losing, 43, 44
    available by route named only, 44.
    advertisements on, 44, 45
SEAT,
    passenger's right to retain, 100.
    luggage on, 100
    when, may be appropriated, 101

SHEEP,
  company's liability for, 77
SMOKING,
  in carriage or on platform, etc , 22
  curious bye law about, 22
  company liable for allowing, when, 23
  misconduct of some smokers, 23
  no carriages for, 22, 23, 34.
SPARK,
  from engine causing fire, 109-111
SPECIAL CONTRACT,
  as to carriage of goods, when valid, 76, 77
SPECIAL PURPOSE,
  train run for, company liable if late, 54.
SPECIAL TRAIN,
  when passenger may take, at company's cost, 52, 53, 61
STATION,
  using ticket for wrong, 24, 25
  passenger carried beyond, 61.
  calling out name of, no invitation to alight, 87
  train failing to stop at, 105
STEPS,
  riding on, 20
STRAP,
  window, penalty for cutting, 34
SUNDAY,
  getting drink on in refreshment-room, 106-108
SUPERIOR CLASS,
  when actionable to put passengers of inferior into, 16
  using ticket for, how passenger should act, 31-34

TENDER,
  of fare, 7.
THEFT,
  of goods by servant, company liable when, 75, 76
  by finder of lost article, what is, 103
TICKET,
  passenger not bound to give up, 2, 24, 44
  passenger without, not liable to pay fare from where train
    started, 7

TICKET—*continued*,

    passenger without, what to do, 7

    lost, what to do, 7

    given up in error, what to do, 8

    wrong part given up, what to do, 8

    return, not available after date named, 9

        ,, penalty for transferring, etc , 11.

    issued conditionally at intermediate stations, 12

    defacing, penalty for, 20

    using, for wrong station, 25

    ordinary, company must issue, 54

    cheap, due notice of withdrawal required, 57

    passenger without, company liable for negligence, 90, 91.

    excursion, *see* "Excursion Ticket"

    season, *see* "Season Ticket"

TIME TABLES,

    need not be issued, 55

    if issued, form a contract, 55

    when notice of change in, required, 55, 56

    train shown in, not run, 56

TRAIN,

    overcrowding, 14, 15

    passenger robbed in, 15

    in motion, entering or leaving, 21

    unpunctuality of, 46-48

    special, when passenger may take, 52, 53

    advertised, not run, 56

    discontinued after time table issued, 58

    passenger put into wrong, 59, 61

    divided *in route*, passenger in wrong part, 61

    not coming properly to platform, 87

    a public place, when, 98

    not stopping at station, 105

    wrecking, 112

TRESPASS,

    company can prosecute for, 104

    question of right, justices can decide, 104, 105

    by cattle, company must fence against, 111

UNCLAIMED PROPERTY,

    to whom it belongs, 101-103

UNPUNCTUALITY,
    general regulations, 46, 47
    when company liable for, 47, 48, 54.
    company not liable if due to fog, etc., 48.
USING TICKET,
    for wrong station, 24-30
    for superior class, 31 34

VALUABLES,
    carriage of, 73
    duty of finder of, 103
VENTILATION,
    in railway carriages, 108, 109

WAITING ROOM,
    smoking in, 22
WINDOW,
    breaking carriage, 34-36.
    scratching, 34
    strap, cutting, 34
    passengers' rights as to opening, etc , 108, 109.
WORDS,
    offensive, writing on carriage, etc , 37
WRECKING TRAIN, 112.
WRITING,
    offensive, on carriage, etc , 37
WRONG NAME, ETC.,
    passenger giving, 5
WRONG TRAIN,
    passenger put into, 59 61

THE ABERDEEN UNIVERSITY PRESS LIMITED